THE LOEB CLASSICAL LIBRARY

FOUNDED BY JAMES LOEB

EDITED BY

G. P. GOOLD

PREVIOUS EDITORS

MARTIAL
III

LCL 480

MARTIAL

EPIGRAMS

EDITED AND TRANSLATED BY

D. R. SHACKLETON BAILEY

VOLUME III

HARVARD UNIVERSITY PRESS

CAMBRIDGE, MASSACHUSETTS

LONDON, ENGLAND

1993

Library of Congress Cataloging-in-Publication Data

Martial.
Epigrams / edited and translated by D. R. Shackleton Bailey.
p.   cm. — (Loeb classical library)
Translation of: Epigrammata.
Includes bibliographical references and index.
ISBN 0–674–99555–4 (v. 1).   ISBN 0–674–99556–2 (v. 2).
ISBN 0–674–99529–5 (v. 3).
1. Martial—Translations into English.
2. Epigrams. Latin—Translations into English.
3. Occasional verse, Latin—Translations into English.
I. Shackleton Bailey, D. R. (David Roy), 1917– .
II. Title.   III. Series: Loeb classical library; L094, L095, L480
PA6502.B35   1993   92–8234
878'.0102—dc20   CIP

Typeset by Chiron, Inc, Cambridge, Massachusetts.
Printed in Great Britain by St Edmundsbury Press Ltd,
Bury St Edmunds, Suffolk, on acid-free paper.
Bound by Hunter & Foulis Ltd, Edinburgh, Scotland.

CONTENTS

EPIGRAMS
BOOKS XI–XIV

LIBER XI

1

Quo tu, quo, liber otiose, tendis
cultus Sidone non cotidiana?
numquid Parthenium videre? certe:
vadas et redeas inevolutus.
5 libros non legit ille sed libellos;
nec Musis vacat, aut suis vacaret.
ecquid te satis aestimas beatum,
contingunt tibi si manus minores?
vicini pete porticum Quirini:
10 turbam non habet otiosiorem
Pompeius vel Agenoris puella,
vel primae dominus levis carinae.
sunt illic duo tresve qui revolvant
nostrarum tineas ineptiarum,
15 sed cum sponsio fabulaeque lassae
de Scorpo fuerint et Incitato.

2

BOOK XI

1

Where, where are you going, holiday book, dressed
in purple not of every day? Is it to see Parthenius?
To be sure. You would go and return unrolled. He
does not read books but petitions,[a] and has no time
for the Muses, else he would have time for his own.
Do you think yourself sufficiently happy if you fall
into lesser hands? Then make for the colonnade of
our neighbor Quirinus.[b] Not Pompey, nor Agenor's
girl, nor the fickle captain of the first ship[c] has an
idler crowd. There are two or three there to unroll
the bookworms breeding in my trifles, but only
when the betting and gossiping about Scorpus and
Incitatus is played out.

[a] Addressed to the Emperor.

[b] The temple of Quirinus near M.'s house; cf. 10.58.10.

[c] The references are respectively to the Porticus Pom
peii (cf. 2.14.10); the Porticus Europae (cf. 2.14.15); and
the Porticus Argonautarum (cf. 2.14.6). Jason is called
levis because of his conduct to Medea.

2

Triste supercilium durique severa Catonis
    frons et aratoris filia Fabricia
et personati fastus et regula morum,
    quidquid et in tenebris non sumus, ite foras.
5 clamant ecce mei 'Io Saturnalia' versus:
    et licet et sub te praeside, Nerva, libet.
lectores tetrici salebrosum ediscite Santram:
    nil mihi vobiscum est: iste liber meus est.

3

Non urbana mea tantum Pipleide gaudent
    otia nec vacuis auribus ista damus,
sed meus in Geticis ad Martia signa pruinis
    a rigidio teritur centurione liber,
5 dicitur et nostros cantare Britannia versus.
    quid prodest? nescit sacculus ista meus.
at quam victuras poteramus pangere chartas
    quantaque Pieria proelia flare tuba,
cum pia reddiderint Augustum numina terris,
10   et Maecenatem si tibi, Roma, darent!

2.2 Fabricia *P. Wagner* : -cii βγ   6 libet . . . licet ς

4

2

Gloomy brow and stern countenance of unbending
Cato and Fabricia, the plowman's daughter,[a] and
pride in its mask, and moral code, and everything
that in the dark we are not: out you go. Look, my
verses shout "Hurrah for the Saturnalia!" Under
your rule, Nerva,[b] it's allowed, and it's our pleasure.
You austere readers learn jerky[c] Santra by heart, I
am not concerned with you. This book is mine.

3

Not alone does Rome's leisure rejoice in my Pipleis,
nor do I give these pieces only to empty ears. My
book is thumbed by hard centurions beside Mars'
standards in Getic frosts, and Britain is said to
recite my verses. What's the use? My purse knows
nothing of all that. Ah, but what immortal pages
could I indite, what mighty battles could I blow on
Pierian trumpet, if, in restoring Augustus' divinity[d]
to earth, the gods in their benevolence had given
Rome a Maecenas too!

[a] Fabricius' daughters were given dowries by the senate
because of his poverty. The manuscript reading *Fabricii*
contravenes M.'s practice of avoiding the genitive ending in
-*ii*. *Cybii* in 11.27.3 and 11.31.14 should not count as an
exception; see Housman, 943.

[b] Who succeeded Domitian in October of A.D. 96, this
book being published at the Saturnalia in December.

[c] Cf. 11.90.2.

[d] In the person of Nerva.

4

Sacra laresque Phrygum quos Troiae maluit heres
    quam rapere arsuras Laomedontis opes,
scriptus et aeterno nunc primum Iuppiter auro
    et soror et summi filia tota patris,
5 et qui purpureis iam tertia nomina fastis,
    Iane, refers Nervae; vos precor ore pio:
hunc omnes servate ducem, servate senatum;
    moribus hic vivat principis, ille suis.

5

Tanta tibi est recti reverentia, Caesar, et aequi
    quanta Numae fuerat: sed Numa pauper erat.
ardua res haec est, opibus non tradere mores
    et, cum tot Croesos viceris, esse Numam.
5 si redeant veteres, ingentia nomina, patres,
    Elysium liceat si vacuare nemus,
te colet invictus pro libertate Camillus,
    aurum Fabricius te tribuente volet,
te duce gaudebit Brutus, tibi Sulla cruentus
10   imperium tradet, cum positurus erit,

---

[a] Aeneas.

[b] I.e. the wealth of Troy.

[c] Some representation of Jupiter placed by Nerva in the temple on the Capitol. *Aeterno* = never again to be destroyed by fire.

[d] Juno and Minerva, the latter being "wholly his" as having sprung from his head.

[e] Nerva being consul for the third time. The consular

4

Sacred emblems and household gods of the Phrygi-
ans, which Troy's heir[a] chose to rescue leaving
Laomedon's wealth[b] to the flames, and Jupiter, now
for the first time depicted in everlasting gold,[c] and
you the sister and you the daughter,[d] wholly his, of
the supreme Father, and you, Janus, who now for
the third time bring back the name of Nerva to the
purple annals,[e] to you in piety I pray: preserve you
all this our Leader, preserve the senate; let it live by
its prince's code, he by his own.

5

Caesar, your reverence for right and justice is no
less than Numa's was; but Numa was a poor man.
It is a hard thing not to sacrifice morals to wealth
and to be Numa when you are richer than many a
Croesus. If the fathers[f] of old, those mighty names,
were to return and the Elysian grove could be emp-
tied, Camillus, unconquered champion of freedom,[g]
would be your courtier, and Fabricius[h] would accept
your proffered gold; Brutus would rejoice to be
under your leadership, bloodstained Sulla when

records were kept in the temple of Janus: cf. 8.66.11. "Pur-
ple" either = consular, from the consul's purple gown, or
referring to actual purple lettering in the volume; cf.
12.29.5.
[f] I.e. senators.
[g] Cf. 1.24.3.
[h] Who refused the presents of Pyrrhus, king of Epirus.

et te privato cum Caesare Magnus amabit,
    donabit totas et tibi Crassus opes.
ipse quoque infernis revocatus Ditis ab umbris
    si Cato reddatur, Caesarianus erit.

6

Unctis falciferi senis diebus,
regnator quibus imperat fritillus,
versu ludere non laborioso
permittis, puto, pilleata Roma.
5 risisti; licet ergo, non vetamur.
pallentes procul hinc abite curae;
quidquid venerit obvium loquamur
morosa sine cogitatione.
misce dimidios, puer, trientes,
10 quales Pythagoras dabat Neroni,
misce, Dindyme, sed frequentiores:
possum nil ego sobrius; bibenti
succurrent mihi quindecim poetae.
da nunc basia, sed Catulliana:
15 quae si tot fuerint quot ille dixit,
donabo tibi Passerem Catulli.

about to resign his power would hand it over to you, Magnus[a] would love you along with Caesar, a private citizen, and Crassus give you all his wealth. If even Cato himself, recalled from the nether shades of Dis, were to be returned to us, he wold be a Caesarian.

6

On the sumptuous feast days of the old Scythe-bearer,[b] over which King Dice-box rules, methinks you allow me, cap-clad[c] Rome, to sport in toil-free verse. You smile. Permission granted then, I am not forbidden. Pale cares, get you far hence. Whatever comes my way, let me out with it and no moody meditation. Boy, mix me bumpers half and half, such as Pythagoras used to give to Nero, mix them, Dindymus, and not too long between them. I can do nothing sober, but when I drink, fifteen poets will come to my aid. Give me kisses, Catullian kisses.[d] If they shall be as many as he said, I will give you Catullus' Sparrow.[e]

[a] Pompey the Great (Cn. Pompeius Magnus).

[b] Saturn.

[c] The *pilleus*, or cap of liberty worn by manumitted slaves (cf. 2.68.4), was also generally worn at the Saturnalia. It was a symbol of license.

[d] Cf. Catull. 5.7–9 and 3.

[e] Cf. 1.7.3n. Clearly with an obscene double sense here, but that is M.'s contribution. Catullus meant no such thing, nor is M. likely to have thought he did.

7

Iam certe stupido non dices, Paula, marito,
  ad moechum quotiens longius ire voles,
'Caesar in Albanum iussit me mane venire,
  Caesar Circeios.' iam stropha talis abît.
5 Penelopae licet esse tibi sub principe Nerva:
  sed prohibet scabies ingeniumque vetus.
infelix, quid ages? aegram simulabis amicam?
  haerebit dominae vir comes ipse suae,
ibit et ad fratrem tecum matremque patremque.
10   quas igitur fraudes ingeniosa paras?
diceret hystericam se forsitan altera moecha
  in Sinuessano velle sedere lacu.
quanto tu melius, quotiens placet ire fututum,
  quae verum mavis dicere, Paula, viro!

8

Lassa quod hesterni spirant opobalsama dracti,
  ultima quod curvo quae cadit aura croco;
poma quod hiberna maturescentia capsa,
  arbore quod verna luxuriosus ager;
5 de Palatinis dominae quod Serica prelis,
  sucina virginea quod regelata manu;
amphora quod nigri, sed longe, fracta Falerni,
  quod qui Sicanias detinet hortus apes;

8.1 dracti *Housman* : drauci T$\beta\gamma$

---

[a] M. had presumably known this all along, which
makes the preceding speculations inapposite. But the
reader gets his surprise.

10

7

Now at least, Paula, you will not be saying to your
fool of a husband, whenever you want to go to a
lover at a distance: "Caesar has commanded me to
go to Alba tomorrow morning. Caesar has com-
manded me to Circeii." The day for such a ruse has
gone by. Under Nerva's rule you can be Penelope,
but your itch, your old bent, won't let you. What
will you do, wretched woman? Pretend a sick
friend? Your husband himself will stick to his lady
and accompany you to brother or mother or father.
So, my clever one, what fraud are you hatching?
Perhaps another of your kind might say she was
hysterical and wanted to sit in the waters of
Sinuessa. How much better you manage, Paula!
Whenever you have a mind to go for a fuck, you
prefer to tell your husband the truth.[a]

8

Perfume of faded balsam in yesterday's vases; last
aroma that falls from a curving jet of saffron;[b] scent
of apples ripening in their winter box, or of a field
luxuriant with spring foliage, or of silks from our
Lady's[c] Palatine presses, or of amber warmed in a
girl's hand, or of a jar of black Falernian broken, but
a long way off, or of a garden keeping Sicanian bees;

[b] Cf. 5.25.7n.
[c] The Emperor's wife.

11

quod Cosmi redolent alabastra focique deorum,
10   quod modo divitibus lapsa corona comis —
singula quid dicam? non sunt satis; omnia misce:
   hoc fragrant pueri basia mane mei.
scire cupis nomen? si propter basia, dicam.
   iurasti. nimium scire, Sabine, cupis.

9

Clarus fronde Iovis, Romani fama cothurni,
   spirat Apellea redditus arte Memor.

10

Contulit ad saturas ingentia pectora Turnus.
   cur non ad Memoris carmina? frater erat.

11

Tolle, puer, calices tepidique toreumata Nili
   et mihi secura pocula trade manu
trita patrum labris et tonso pura ministro;
   anticus mensis restituatur honor.
5 te potare decet gemma, qui Mentora frangis
   in scaphium moechae, Sardanapalle, tuae.

---

^a He swears too eagerly, and M. withholds the name; so
better not translate "you want to know too much."
^b Cf. 4.1.6.

12

odor of Cosmus' alabaster boxes and the hearths of the gods, or of a garland just fallen from richly pomaded locks—why speak of this or that? They are not enough. Mix them all together: such is the fragrance of my boy's morning kisses. Do you wish to know his name? If it's only on account of the kisses, I'll tell you. You swear it. You are too anxious to know,[a] Sabinus.

9

Memor, illustrious in Jupiter's leaves,[b] fame of the Roman buskin, breathes, recalled by Apelles' art.[c]

10

Turnus brought a mighty genius to writing satires. Why not to Memor's kind of poetry? He was Memor's brother.

11

Boy, remove the goblets, the chased chalices of warm Nile, and with nothing to fear hand me cups worn by our forebears' lips, plain, with a close-cropped bearer to go with them; let their old-time dignity be restored to our boards. It is for you, Sardanapallus,[d] to drink from jewels, you who break a Mentor to make a chamber pot for your mistress.

[c] The art of painting.
[d] See Appendix B.

12

Ius tibi natorum vel septem, Zoile, detur,
dum matrem nemo det tibi, nemo patrem.

13

Quisquis Flaminiam teris, viator,
noli nobile praeterire marmor.
urbis deliciae salesque Nili,
ars et gratia, lusus et voluptas,
5   Romani decus et dolor theatri
atque omnes Veneres Cupidinesque
hoc sunt condita, quo Paris, sepulchro.

14

Heredes, nolite brevem sepelire colonum:
nam terra est illi quantulacumque gravis.

15

Sunt chartae mihi quas Catonis uxor
et quas horribiles legant Sabinae:
hic totus volo rideat libellus
et sit nequior omnibus libellis,
5   qui vino madeat nec erubescat
pingui sordidus esse Cosmiano,
ludat cum pueris, amet puellas,
nec per circuitus loquatur illam,
ex qua nascimur, omnium parentem,
10 quam sanctus Numa mentulam vocabat.

12

You are welcome to the Right of Children, even seven, Zoilus, so long as nobody gives you a mother or a father.

13

Traveller, be you who you may, that tread the Flaminian Way, do not pass this noble marble by. The city's darling, the wit of Nile, art and grace, play and pleasure, the ornament and sorrow of the Roman stage, and all Venuses and Cupids are buried here in Paris' tomb.

14

Heirs, do not bury the little farmer; for earth, however exiguous, is heavy to him.[a]

15

I have writings that Cato's wife and severe Sabine dames might read. But I want all of this little book to laugh and be naughtier than all little books. Let it be soaked in wine nor blush for the stains of rich Cosmian pomade, let it play with the boys, love the girls, and name outright that from which we are born, the universal parent, which holy Numa used

[a] Appendix A.

versus hos tamen esse tu memento
Saturnalicios, Apollinaris:
mores non habet hic meos libellus.

16

Qui gravis es nimium, potes hinc iam, lector, abire
    quo libet: urbanae scripsimus ista togae;
iam mea Lampsacio lascivit pagina versu
    et Tartesiaca concrepat aera manu.
5 o quotiens rigida pulsabis pallia vena,
    sis gravior Curio Fabricioque licet!
tu quoque nequitias nostri lususque libelli
    uda, puella, leges, sis Patavina licet.
erubuit posuitque meum Lucretia librum,
10   sed coram Bruto; Brute, recede: leget.

17

Non omnis nostri nocturna est pagina libri:
    invenies et quod mane, Sabine, legas.

18

Donasti, Lupe, rus sub urbe nobis;
    sed rus est mihi maius in fenestra.
rus hoc dicere, rus potes vocare?
    in quo ruta facit nemus Dianae,

---

[a] I.e. Priapic.
[b] Like a dancing girl from Gades.
[c] *Uda* does not refer to drinking; see *SB*[1].

to call "cock." But remember, Apollinaris, that these
are Saturnalian verses. This little book does not
have my morals.

16

Too serious reader, you may leave at this point and
go where you please. I wrote those pieces for the
city gown; now my page frolics with verse of
Lampsacus[a] and clashes the cymbals with Tartesian
hand.[b] Oh, how often will you strike your garment
with rigid member, though you be graver than
Curius and Fabricius! You also, my girl, will not be
dry[c] as you read the naughty jests of my little book,
though you come from Patavium.[d] Lucretia[e]
blushed and put my book aside, but that was in
front of Brutus. Brutus, withdraw: she will read.

17

Not every page in my book is of the night. You will
also find, Sabinus, matter to read in the morning.[f]

18

Lupus, you have given me a country property close
to Rome, but I have a bigger property in my window.
Can you speak of this as a property, call this a pro-
perty? In it a rue plant makes a grove of Diana, the

[d] A town (modern Padua) with a reputation for strict
morals; cf. Pliny *Epist.* 1.14.6.
[e] Type of wifely virtue.
[f] When you are sober.

5   argutae tegit ala quod cicadae,
     quod formica die comedit uno,
     clusae cui folium rosae corona est;
     in quo non magis invenitur herba
     quam Cosmi folium piperve crudum;
10 in quo nec cucumis iacere rectus
     nec serpens habitare tota possit.
     urucam male pascit hortus unam,
     consumpto moritur culix salicto,
     et talpa est mihi fossor atque arator.
15 non boletus hiare, non mariscae
     ridere aut violae patere possunt.
     finis mus populatur et colono
     tamquam sus Calydonius timetur,
     et sublata volantis ungue Procnes
20 in nido seges est hirundinino;
     et cum stet sine falce mentulaque,
     non est dimidio locus Priapo.
     vix implet cocleam peracta messis,
     et mustum nuce condimus picata.
25 errasti, Lupe, littera sed una:
     nam quo tempore praedium dedisti,
     mallem tu mihi prandium dedisses.

wing of a shrill cricket covers it, an ant eats it up in a single day, for it the petal of a rosebud is a garland. Grass is not found therein any more than Cosmus' leaf[a] or green pepper. A cucumber cannot lie straight in it and a snake cannot live in it at full length. The garden hardly feeds a single caterpillar, and a gnat dies when it has consumed the willow, and the mole is my ditcher and plowman. A mushroom can't gape, figs can't split,[b] violets can't open. A mouse ravages the borders and the farmer fears him like the Caledonian boar. The crop is in a swallow's nest, lifted up by flying Procne's[c] claw. And there isn't room enough for half a Priapus, though he stand without sickle and cock. The harvest[d] when completed hardly fills a snail-shell and we lay down the must in a tarred nut. You made a mistake, Lupus, but only of one letter. When you gave me land (*praedium*), I'd rather you had given me lunch (*prandium*).

[a] Herbs used for the perfume called *foliatum*; cf. 11.27.9n.

[b] Lit. "laugh."

[c] The swallow, which however lives on insects and never holds food in its claws (Ker).

[d] The difference between "harvest" (*messis*) and "crop" (*seges*, v. 20) is not apparent.

19

Quaeris cur nolim te ducere, Galla? diserta es.
 saepe soloecismum mentula nostra facit.

20

Caesaris Augusti lascivos, livide, versus
 sex lege, qui tristis verba Latina legis:
'quod futuit Glaphyran Antonius, hanc mihi poenam
 Fulvia constituit, se quoque uti futuam.
5 Fulviam ego ut futuam? quid si me Manius oret
 pedicem? faciam? non puto, si sapiam.
"aut futue; aut pugnemus" ait. quid quod mihi vita
 carior est ipsa mentula? signa canant!'
absolvis lepidos nimirum, Auguste, libellos,
10 qui scis Romana simplicitate loqui.

21

Lydia tam laxa est equitis quam culus aeni,
 quam celer arguto qui sonat aere trochus,
quam rota transmisso totiens intacta petauro,
 quam vetus a crassa calceus udus aqua,

21.3 intacta T : inpa- $\beta\gamma$

ᵃ Cf. Juv. 6.456 *soloecismum liceat fecisse marito*, of the
husband of a learned wife. But here M. adds an obscene
sense.

ᵇ If genuine, they will come from a collection of epi-
grams by Augustus, not necessarily published by himself.

ᶜ Fulvia is angry with her husband Antony—and pun-
ishes Caesar (cf. *SB*¹).

ᵈ The war in view is not of course that between Caesar

19

You ask me why I don't want to marry you, Galla?
You are so literate. My cock often commits a
solecism.[a]

20

Malignant one, you who read Latin words with a
sour face, read six wanton verses of Caesar
Augustus:[b] "Because Antony fucks Glaphyra, Fulvia
determined to punish *me* by making me fuck her in
turn.[c] I fuck Fulvia? What if Manius begged me to
sodomize him, would I do it? I think not, if I were in
my right mind. 'Either fuck me or let us fight,' says
she. Ah, but my cock is dearer to me than life itself.
Let the trumpets sound."[d] Augustus, you surely
absolve my witty little books, knowing how to speak
with Roman candor.

21

Lydia is as spacious as the arse of a brazen
horseman,[e] as a swift hoop, noisy with its clattering
bronze,[f] as the wheel through which the acrobat
often leaps without touching it,[g] as an old shoe

(Octavian) and Antony, but the Perusine War of 41–40 B.C.
between the former and Antony's brother Lucius backed by
Fulvia.

[e] I.e. equestrian statue, the rump being the horse's. Cf.
4.67.8n.

[f] Rings were attached to boys' hoops; cf. 14.169.

[g] Explained by Housman on Manil. 5.442.

5   quam quae rara vagos expectant retia turdos,
        quam Pompeiano vela negata Noto,
quam quae de pthisico lapsa est armilla cinaedo,
        culcita Leuconico quam viduata suo,
quam veteres bracae Brittonis pauperis, et quam
10   turpe Ravennatis guttur onocrotali.
hanc in piscina dicor futuisse marina.
        nescio; piscinam me futuisse puto.

22

Mollia quod nivei duro teris ore Galaesi
    basia, quod nudo cum Ganymede iaces,
— quis negat? — hoc nimium est. sed sit satis; inguina saltem
    parce fututrici sollicitare manu.
5   levibus in pueris plus haec quam mentula peccat
    et faciunt digiti praecipitantque virum:
inde tragus celeresque pili mirandaque matri
    barba nec in clara balnea luce placent.
divisit natura marem: pars una puellis,
10   una viris genita est. utere parte tua.

---

[a] They could not be spread in a strong wind; cf. 9.38.6;
14.29.2. It is also possible to take *Noto* as dative, "denied
to the wind (by the management)," but this accords less
well with the other passages. See *SB*[1].

[b] Described by Pliny, *N.H.* 10.131. By "throat" M.
means the large pouch under the mandibles (the *alterius
uteri genus* of Pliny's description), where the pelican stores
its catch of fish.

22

soaked in muddy water, as the wide-meshed nets
that wait for stray thrushes, as the awnings denied
by the South Wind[a] in Pompey's theater, as an
armlet that slipped from a consumptive catamite, as
a mattress divorced from its Leuconian stuffing, as
the old breeches of a pauper Briton, and as the ugly
throat of a pelican[b] of Ravenna. I am said to have
fucked her in a marine fishpond. I don't know; I
think I fucked the fishpond.

22

That you rub snow-white Galaesus' soft kisses with
your hard mouth, that you lie with naked
Ganymede[c]—it's too much, who denies it? But let it
be enough. Refrain at least from stirring their
groins with your fornicating hand. Where smooth
boys are concerned, the hand is a worse offender
than the cock; the fingers make and precipitate
manhood. Hence come the goat and rapid hairs and
a beard to make a mother marvel, hence baths in
broad daylight displease. Nature divided the male:
one part was created for girls, one for men. Use
your part.

[c] Not "a naked Ganymede." The name, fictitious of
course, must be personal like Galaesus. "Ganymedes" was
in actual use as a personal name, but naturally M. chose it
here because of its associations. Galaesus suggests the
softness and whiteness of the wool of the Tarentine dis-
trict; cf. 5.37.2; 12.63.3.

23

Nubere Sila mihi nulla non lege parata est;
  sed Silam nulla ducere lege volo.
cum tamen instaret, 'deciens mihi dotis in auro
  sponsa dabis' dixi. 'quid minus esse potest?'
5 'nec futuam quamvis prima te nocte maritus,
  communis tecum nec mihi lectus erit;
complectarque meam, nec tu prohibebis, amicam,
  ancillam mittes et mihi iussa tuam.
te spectante dabit nobis lasciva minister
10 basia, sive meus sive erit ille tuus.
ad cenam venies, sed sic divisa recumbes
  ut non tangantur pallia nostra tuis.
oscula rara dabis nobis et non dabis ultro,
  nec quasi nupta dabis sed quasi mater anus.
15 si potes ista pati, si nil perferre recusas,
  invenies qui te ducere, Sila, velit.'

24

Dum te prosequor et domum reduco,
  aurem dum tibi praesto garrienti,
et quidquid loqueris facisque laudo,
  quot versus poterant, Labulle, nasci!
5 hoc damnum tibi non videtur esse,
  si quod Roma legit, requirit hospes,
non deridet eques, tenet senator,
  laudat causidicus, poeta carpit,
propter te perit? hoc, Labulle, verum est?

23.4 quid ... potest? *Siliae tribuit SB*[1]   24.4 *et* 9
labulle *γ* : fa- *β et sic alibi*

23

Sila is ready to marry me on any terms; but on no
terms do I want to marry Sila. However, when she
insisted, I said: "At our betrothal you will give me a
million by way of dowry in gold." "What could be
more reasonable?" "And I shall not fuck you when I
am your husband, even on our wedding night, nei-
ther shall I share my bed with you. I shall embrace
my mistress, and you will not forbid it; when bidden,
you will send me your maid. The page will give me
lascivious kisses before your eyes, whether he's
mine or yours. You will come to dinner, but you will
recline apart from me, so that my mantle is not
touched by yours. You will kiss me seldom, and only
on request, and not as a bride but as an elderly
mother. If you can stomach all that, if there's noth-
ing you won't put up with—you'll find somebody wil-
ling to marry you, Sila."

24

In the time I escort you out and bring you back
home, in the time I lend an ear to your chatter and
praise whatever you say or do, how many verses,
Labullus, could have come into being! Do you think
it no loss that what Rome reads and strangers
demand, what knights do not scorn, senators know
by heart, barristers praise, poets criticize, goes to
waste because of you? Is this fair, Labullus? Would

10 hoc quisquam ferat? ut tibi tuorum
   sit maior numerus togatulorum,
   librorum mihi sit minor meorum?
   triginta prope iam diebus una est
   nobis pagina vix peracta. sic fit
15 cum cenare domi poeta non vult.

25

Illa salax nimium nec paucis nota puellis
   stare Lino desît mentula. lingua, cave.

26

O mihi grata quies, o blanda, Telesphore, cura,
   qualis in amplexu non fuit ante meo,
basia da nobis vetulo, puer, uda Falerno,
   pocula da labris facta minora tuis.
5 addideris super haec Veneris si gaudia vera,
   esse negem melius cum Ganymede Iovi.

27

Ferreus es, si stare potest tibi mentula, Flacce,
   cum te sex cyathos orat amica gari,
vel duo frusta rogat cybii tenuemve lacertum
   nec dignam toto se botryone putat;
5 cui portat gaudens ancilla paropside rubra
   allecem, sed quam protinus illa voret;
aut cum perfricuit frontem posuitque pudorem,
   sucida palliolo vellera quinque petit.

anyone stand for it? So that the number of your little clients be larger, should the number of my books be smaller? In almost thirty days I have finished scarce a page. So it goes when a poet does not want to dine at home.

25

That over-active cock, well known to girls not a few, has ceased to stand for Linus. Tongue, look out!

26

Telesphorus, my welcome repose and beguiling care, the like of whom was never before in my arms, give me kisses, boy, wet with old Falernian, give me cups made smaller by your lips. If beyond this you add the true joys of Venus, I would say that Jupiter is no better off with Ganymede.

27

You are made of iron, Flaccus, if your cock can stand when your mistress begs you for half a pint of garum or asks for two pieces of tunny or a meagre mackerel and thinks herself unworthy of a whole bunch of grapes; one to whom her maid delightedly carries fish-sauce on a red platter for her to devour immediately; or, when she has rubbed her forehead and laid modesty aside, one who petitions for five greasy fleeces to make a small mantle. Let *my* mistress on the other hand demand a pound of foliatum[a] or

---

[a] The *foliatum* or *nardinum* was a compound of nard, myrrh, and other aromatic herbs; cf. Pliny *N.H.* 13.15.

at mea me libram foliati poscat amica,
10   aut virides gemmas sardonychasve pares,
nec nisi prima velit de Tusco Serica vico,
    aut centum aureolos sic velut aera roget.
nunc tu velle putas haec me donare puellae?
    nolo, sed his ut sit digna puella volo.

28

Invasit medici Nasica phreneticus Eucti
    et percidit Hylan. hic, puto, sanus erat.

29

Languida cum vetula tractare virilia dextra
    coepisti, iugulor pollice, Phylli, tuo.
iam cum me murem, cum me tua lumina dicis,
    horis me refici vix puto posse decem.
5 blanditias nescis: 'dabo' dic 'tibi milia centum
    et dabo Setini iugera certa soli;
accipe vina, domum, pueros, chrysendeta, mensas.'
    nil opus est digitis: sic mihi, Phylli, frica.

30

Os male causidicis et dicis olere poetis.
    sed fellatori, Zoile, peius olet.

29.3 iam SB^1 : nam T$\beta\gamma$ 6 certa T : culta $\beta\gamma$

green gems or matching sardonyxes; let her want none but the finest silks from Tuscan Street, or let her ask me for a hundred gold pieces as if they were copper. Do you now suppose that I am minded to give my girl such things? I am not, but I wish my girl to be worthy of them.

28

Nasica, a mental case, assaulted Doctor Euctus' Hylas and sodomized him. I fancy he was sane.

29

When you start stroking my slack parts with your ancient hand, I am slaughtered by your thumb, Phyllis; and when you go on to call me "mouse" or "light of my eyes," I hardly think I can recover in ten hours. You don't know how to cajole. Say "I'll give you a hundred thousand and I'll give you some reliable[a] acres of Setine soil; take wine, a house, boys, gold-inlaid dishes, tables." No need for fingers. That's the way to rub for my money, Phyllis.

30

You say that barristers' mouths and poets' mouths smell bad.[b] But a sucker's mouth, Zoilus, smells worse.

[a] Yielding an assured return; so Pliny *Epist.* 4.6.3 *certa et fructuosa praedia.*
[b] Both hold forth at length.

31

Atreus Caecilius cucurbitarum:
sic illas quasi filios Thyestae
in partes lacerat secatque mille.
gustu protinus has edes in ipso,
5   has prima feret alteraque cena.
has cena tibi tertia reponet,
hinc seras epidipnidas parabit.
hinc pistor fatuas facit placentas,
hinc et multiplices struit tabellas
10   et notas caryotidas theatris.
hinc exit varium coco minutal,
hinc lentem positam fabamque credas;
boletos imitatur et botellos,
et caudam cybii brevesque maenas.
15   hinc bellarius experitur artes,
ut condat vario vafer sapore
in rutae folium Capelliana.
sic implet gabatas paropsidasque,
et leves scutulas cavasque lances.
20   hoc lautum vocat, hoc putat venustum,
unum ponere ferculis tot assem.

31.12 hinc *scripsi* : ut $\beta\gamma$ 15 bellarius SB^3 : ce-
$\beta\gamma$ 18 paropsidas *Housman* : -des $\beta\gamma$

31

Caecilius is the Atreus of pumpkins. He tears and cuts them into a thousand pieces as though they were sons of Thyestes. You will eat them straight off in the hors d'oeuvres itself, he will bring them in the first and second courses and serve them up again in the third, he will manufacture savories out of them at the end. His baker makes tasteless cakes out of them, constructs multi-layered tablets out of them and dates familiar to theaters. Hence his cook makes various mincemeats emerge, hence are served what you would take for lentils and beans. He imitates[a] mushrooms and sausages and a tunny's tail and little sprats. With them the confectioner tries out his skills, cunningly putting variously flavored Capelliana[b] into a rue-leaf. So he fills side dishes and platters and polished saucers and hollow plates. This he calls elegant, this he thinks charming—to serve[c] one penny piece in so many courses.

[a] Caecilius or the cook? Perhaps read *imitantur*, "they (the pumpkins) imitate."

[b] Probably some sort of sweetmeat called after its inventor.

[c] *ponere* can also mean "lay out, invest."

32

Nec toga nec focus est nec tritus cimice lectus
　　nec tibi de bibula sarta palude teges,
nec puer aut senior, nulla est ancilla nec infans,
　　nec sera nec clavis nec canis atque calix.
5　tu tamen affectas, Nestor, dici atque videri
　　pauper et in populo quaeris habere locum.
mentiris vanoque tibi blandiris honore.
　　non est paupertas, Nestor, habere nihil.

33

Saepius ad palmam prasinus post fata Neronis
　　pervenit et victor praemia plura refert.
i nunc, livor edax, dic te cessisse Neroni:
　　vicit nimirum non Nero, sed prasinus.

34

Aedes emit Aper, sed quas nec noctua vellet
　　esse suas; adeo nigra vetusque casa est.
vicinos illi nitidos Maro possidet hortos.
　　cenabit belle, non habitabit Aper.

35

　　Ignotos mihi cum voces trecentos,
　　quare non veniam vocatus ad te
　　miraris quererisque litigasque.
　　solus ceno, Fabulle, non libenter.

34.3 nitidos Tβ : -dus γ

---

[a] Imitated from Catull. 23.1–2.

32

You don't have a gown or a fireplace or a bug-trodden bed or a patched up mat of thirsty rushes or a boy slave or an older one or a maidservant or a baby or a key or a dog or a cup.[a] Yet, Nestor, you aspire to be called and seen as a poor man and seek to have a place in the community. You lie and flatter yourself with a false honor. It is not poverty, Nestor, to have nothing.

33

Since Nero's death the Green often wins the race and brings back many prizes of victory. Go now, gnawing envy,[b] and say you yielded to Nero;[c] for sure, it was not Nero who won, but the Green.

34

Aper bought a house, but one that even an owl would not wish its own—such a dark old cottage. Maro owns a fine suburban property near by. Aper will dine in good style, and lodge in bad.

35

You invite hordes of people I don't know, and you are surprised and indignant and quarrelsome because I don't come to you at your invitation. Fabullus, I don't like dining alone.

[b] I.e. of rival charioteers.
[c] Perhaps with a covert allusion to Domitian, recently dead, whom Juvenal (4.38) calls "the bald Nero."

36

Gaius hanc lucem gemma mihi Iulius alba
    signat, io, votis redditus ecce meis.
desperasse iuvat veluti iam rupta sororum
    fila; minus gaudent qui timuere nihil.
5 Hypne, quid expectas, piger? immortale Falernum
    funde, senem poscunt talia vota cadum:
quincunces et sex cyathos besemque bibamus,
    'Gaius' ut fiat 'Iulius' et 'Proculus'.

37

Zoile, quid tota gemmam praecingere libra
    te iuvat et miserum perdere sardonycha?
anulus iste tuis fuerat modo cruribus aptus:
    non eadem digitis pondera conveniunt.

38

Mulio viginti venît modo milibus, Aule.
    miraris pretium tam grave? surdus erat.

36

Gaius Julius marks this day for me with a white gem,[a] restored, behold him, to my prayers. Hurrah! I am not sorry to have despaired, thinking the Sisters' threads already snapped. They rejoice less who have felt no fear. Hypnus, what are you waiting for, lazybones? Pour immortal Falernian; such vows demand an aged jar. Let us drink five measures and six and eight to make up "Gaius" and "Julius" and "Proculus."[b]

37

Zoilus, why does it please you to surround a jewel with a pound of metal and waste the poor sardonyx? Not long ago that ring would have done for your shanks. The same weights are not appropriate for fingers.[c]

38

A muleteer recently fetched twenty thousand, Aulus. Does such a thumping price surprise you? He was deaf.[d]

[a] A pearl; cf. 8.45.2.
[b] Cf. 9.93.
[c] Zoilus had been a slave, and is now a knight; cf. 3.29.
[d] And so could not hear the talk of those in the carriage: cf. 12.24.8.

39

Cunarum fueras motor, Charideme, mearum
    et pueri custos assiduusque comes.
iam mihi nigrescunt tonsa sudaria barba
    et queritur labris puncta puella meis;
5 sed tibi non crevi; te noster vilicus horret,
    te dispensator, te domus ipsa pavet.
ludere nec nobis nec tu permittis amare;
    nil mihi vis et vis cuncta licere tibi.
corripis, observas, quereris, suspiria ducis,
10   et vix a ferulis temperat ira tua.
si Tyrios sumpsi cultus unxive capillos,
    exclamas 'numquam fecerat ista pater';
et numeras nostros astricta fronte trientes,
    tamquam de cella sit cadus ille tua.
15 desine; non possum libertum ferre Catonem.
    esse virum iam me dicet amica tibi.

40

Formosam Glyceran amat Lupercus
et solus tenet imperatque solus.
quam toto sibi mense non fututam
cum tristis quereretur et roganti
5 causam reddere vellet Aeliano,
respondit Glycerae dolere dentes.

39.10 temperat ira sua (*corr. Beverland*) T : abstinet ira
manum βγ

39

You rocked my cradle, Charidemus, you were my guardian in my boyhood and constant companion. Now the napkins darken with my shaven beard and my girl complains of getting pricked by my lips. But for you I have not grown up. My bailiff goes in terror of you, so does the steward, the house itself dreads you. You don't allow me to play[a] or to fall in love. If you have your way, I am permitted nothing, you are permitted everything. You scold, and spy, and grumble, and sigh; your anger hardly stops short of the cane. If I put on Tyrian clothes or pomade my hair, you exclaim: "Your father never did that." And you count my drinks, knitting your brows, as though the jar came from your own cellar. Stop it. I cannot put up with a Cato for a freedman. My mistress will tell you that I am a man now.

40

Lupercus loves fair Glycera, and he is her sole possessor and master. When he ruefully complained that he had not fucked her in a whole month and tried to explain why to Aelianus, who had asked him, he replied that Glycera had the toothache.[b]

[a] At dice, etc. Or perhaps generally, "have fun."
[b] Which ruled out fellation.

41

Indulget pecori nimium dum pastor Amyntas
    et gaudet fama luxuriaque gregis,
cedentes oneri ramos silvamque pluentem
    vicit, concussas ipse secutus opes.
5 triste nemus dirae vetuit superesse ruinae
    damnavitque rogis noxia ligna pater.
pingues, Lygde, sues habeat vicinus Iollas:
    te satis est nobis annumerare pecus.

42

Vivida cum poscas epigrammata, mortua ponis
    lemmata. qui fieri, Caeciliane, potest?
mella iubes Hyblaea tibi vel Hymettia nasci,
    et thyma Cecropiae Corsica ponis api!

43

Deprensum in puero tetricis me vocibus, uxor,
    corripis et culum te quoque habere refers.
dixit idem quotiens lascivo Iuno Tonanti!
    ille tamen grandi cum Ganymede iacet.
5 incurvabat Hylan posito Tirynthius arcu:
    tu Megaran credis non habuisse natis?

41.3 pluentem *Heinsius* : fl- $\beta\gamma$ 5 ruinae *Rooy* : rapi-
nae $\beta\gamma$ 42.2 qui β : quid Tγ

---

[a] The acorns.
[b] The swineherd of the writer.

41

As Amyntas the swineherd was overfeeding his
beasts, rejoicing in the fame and high condition of
his herd, his weight proved too much for the yield-
ing branches and the raining foliage, and he himself
followed the riches[a] he had shaken down. His
father forbade the sinister tree to survive its dire
collapse, condemning the guilty wood to the pyre.
Let neighbor Iollas have fat pigs, Lygdus.[b] It is
enough for me that you count the herd.

42

You call for lively epigrams, but you propose lifeless
themes. How is it to be done, Caecilianus? You
demand that Hyblaean or Hymettian honey be pro-
duced for you, and you proffer Corsican thyme[c] to
the Cecropian bee.

43

Catching me with a boy, wife, you upbraid me
harshly and point out that you too have an arse.
How often did Juno say the same to her wanton
Thunderer! Nonetheless, he lies with strapping
Ganymede. The Tirynthian used to lay aside his
bow and bend Hylas over: do you think Megara had

[c] Which produced the inferior honey of Corsica: cf.
9.26.4.

torquebat Phoebum Daphne fugitiva: sed illas
    Oebalius flammas iussit abire puer.
Briseis multum quamvis aversa iaceret,
10   Aeacidae proprior levis amicus erat.
parce tuis igitur dare mascula nomina rebus
    teque puta cunnos, uxor, habere duos.

44

Orbus es et locuples et Bruto consule natus:
    esse tibi veras credis amicitias?
sunt verae, sed quas iuvenis, quas pauper habebas.
    qui novus est, mortem diligit ille tuam.

45

Intrasti quotiens inscriptae limina cellae,
    seu puer arrisit sive puella tibi,
contentus non es foribus veloque seraque,
    secretumque iubes grandius esse tibi:
5   oblinitur minimae si qua est suspicio rimae
    punctaque lasciva quae terebrantur acu.
nemo est tam teneri tam sollicitique pudoris
    qui vel pedicat, Canthare, vel futuit.

no buttocks? Fugitive Daphne tormented Phoebus: but the Oebalian boy[a] bade those flames vanish. Though Briseis often lay with her back to Aeacus' son, his smooth friend was closer to him. So kindly don't give masculine names to your belongings, wife, and think of yourself as having two cunts.

44

You are childless and rich and born in Brutus'[b] consulship. Do you believe you have true friendships? You do have them, but only those you used to have when you were young and poor. Any one of your new friends is fond of your death.

45

Whenever you cross the threshold of a labelled cubicle, whether boy or girl has taken your fancy, you are not content with doors and a curtain and a bolt; you demand for yourself a greater measure of secrecy. If there be a suspicion of the smallest chink, any tiny holes bored by a naughty needle, they are plastered over. Nobody is so delicately, so anxiously modest who either sodomizes or fornicates, Cantharus.

[a] Cf. 14.173. According to one version Oebalus, king of Sparta, was Hyacinthus' father, but *Oebalius* probably simply = "Spartan."

[b] The first consul.

46

Iam nisi per somnum non arrigis et tibi, Mevi,
    incipit in medios meiere verpa pedes,
truditur et digitis pannucea mentula lassis
    nec levat extinctum sollicitata caput.
5 quid miseros frustra cunnos culosque lacessis?
    summa petas: illic mentula vivit anus.

47

Omnia femineis quare dilecta catervis
    balnea devitat Lattara? ne futuat.
cur nec Pompeia lentus spatiatur in umbra
    nec petit Inachidos limina? ne futuat.
5 cur Lacedaemonio luteum ceromate corpus
    perfundit gelida Virgine? ne futuat.
cum sic feminei generis contagia vitet,
    cur lingit cunnum Lattara? ne futuat.

48

Silius haec magni celebrat monumenta Maronis,
    iugera facundi qui Ciceronis habet.
heredem dominumque sui tumulive larisve
    non alium mallet nec Maro nec Cicero.

---

[a] Cf. 2.14.10; 11.1.11.
[b] Io = Isis.
[c] Cf. 4.19.5n. Wrestling was cultivated at Sparta.
[d] A pool deriving from the aqueduct; cf. 6.42.18. "Lattara" is said (repetitiously; cf. v. 1) to avoid the baths, which were used by women.

46

You no longer rise, Mevius, except in your sleep, and
your penis begins to piss onto the middle of your
feet; your shrivelled cock is stirred by your weary
fingers and, thus solicited, does not lift its lifeless
head. Why do you vainly pester unfortunate cunts
and arses? You should go for the top. That's where
an aged cock is alive.

47

Why does Lattara avoid all baths patronized by the
feminine cohorts? He doesn't want to fornicate.
Why doesn't he take a leisurely stroll in Pompey's
shade[a] or repair to the threshold of Inachus'
daughter?[b] Doesn't want to fornicate. Why does he
sluice his body, all plastered with Lacedaemonian[c]
mud, with cold Virgin water?[d] Doesn't want to forni-
cate. Since he is at such pains to avoid contact with
the female sex, why does Lattara lick a cunt?
Doesn't want to fornicate.

48

Silius, who possesses the acres of eloquent Cicero,
honors this monument of great Maro.[e] No other heir
and proprietor of his tomb or dwelling would either
Maro or Cicero choose.[f]

[e] For Silius Italicus' cult of Virgil see Pliny *Epist.* 3.7.
[f] Cf. 7.63.

49 (50)

Nulla est hora tibi qua non me, Phylli, furentem
    despolies: tanta calliditate rapis.
nunc plorat speculo fallax ancilla relicto,
    gemma vel a digito vel cadit aure lapis;
5 nunc furtiva lucrifieri bombycina poscunt,
    profertur Cosmi nunc mihi siccus onyx;
amphora nunc petitur nigri cariosa Falerni,
    expiet ut somnos garrula saga tuos;
nunc ut emam grandemve lupum mullumve bilibrem,
10   indixit cenam dives amica tibi.
sit pudor et tandem veri respectus et aequi:
    nil tibi, Phylli, nego; nil mihi, Phylli, nega.

50 (49)

Iam prope desertos cineres et sancta Maronis
    nomina qui coleret pauper et unus erat.
Silius orbatae succurrere censuit umbrae,
    et vatem vates non minor ipse colit.

51

Tanta est quae Titio columna pendet
quantam Lampsaciae colunt puellae.
hic nullo comitante nec molesto
thermis grandibus et suis lavatur.
5 anguste Titius tamen lavatur.

49.5 poscunt *Heinsius* : possunt Tβγ   50 *om.* β
3 orbatae *Ribbeck* : opta- γ   censuit umbrae *Hein-*
sius : cenis et cliabrae (*vel* di-) γ   4 et vatem vates *O.*
L. Richmond ante Hall (et vates vatem) : silius et vatem
γ   minor ipse colit *Heinsius* : minus i- tulit γ

44

49 (50)

Not an hour passes for you, Phyllis, in which you do
not plunder love-crazy me; so cunningly do you rob
me. Now it's your tricky slave girl weeping because
a mirror has been left behind, or a ring falls off your
finger or a stone from your ear. Now stolen silks ask
to yield a profit, now a dry box of Cosmus's is pro-
duced for my benefit, now a crumbling jar of black
Falernian is requested so that a garrulous wise-
woman expiate your dreams,[a] now a rich friend has
invited herself to dinner, so I have to buy a big bass
or a two-pounder mullet. Have some shame, some
respect at last for truth and fair play. I deny you
nothing, Phyllis; deny me nothing, Phyllis.

50 (49)

There was now only one man, a poor man, to honor
Maro's almost forsaken ashes and sacred name.
Silius decided to come to the rescue of his destitute
shade, and honors the poet, no lesser poet he.

51

The column that hangs from Titius rivals in size the
one that the girls of Lampsacus[b] honor. He bathes
in spacious baths, his own baths, with none to
accompany or incommode him. And yet Titius
hasn't room to bathe.

[a] Cf. 7.54.4.
[b] Cf. 11.16.3.

52

Cenabis belle, Iuli Cerialis, apud me;
    condicio est melior si tibi nulla, veni.
octavam poteris servare; lavabimur una:
    scis quam sint Stephani balnea iuncta mihi.
5 prima tibi dabitur ventri lactuca movendo
    utilis, et porris fila resecta suis,
mox vetus et tenui maior cordyla lacerto,
    sed quam cum rutae frondibus ova tegant;
altera non deerunt leni versata favilla,
10   et Velabrensi massa coacta foco,
et quae Picenum senserunt frigus olivae.
    haec satis in gustu. cetera nosse cupis?
mentiar, ut venias: pisces, coloephia, sumen,
    et chortis saturas atque paludis aves,
15 quae nec Stella solet rara nisi ponere cena.
    plus ego polliceor: nil recitabo tibi,
ipse tuos nobis relegas licet usque Gigantas,
    rura vel aeterno proxima Vergilio.

52.9 leni *Heraeus* : tenui βγ   13 coloephia β : conchylia γ

52

You will dine pretty well with me, Julius Cerealis; if you have no better engagement, come along. You will be able to keep the eighth hour.[a] We'll bathe together—you know how close I am to Stephanus' baths. First you'll be given lettuce (a good aperient) and strands cut from their parent leeks;[b] next, an aged tunny, larger than a small mackerel, garnished with eggs and rue leaves. Other eggs, cooked in warm embers, will not be wanting, and a block of cheese congealed over a Velabran[c] hearth, and olives that have felt the frosts of Picenum. So much for the hors d'oeuvres. You want to know the rest? I'll lie to make you come:[d] fish, collops,[e] sow's udder, fat birds of the poultry yard and the marsh, things that even Stella as a rule serves only at a special dinner. I promise something more: I'll recite nothing to you, though *you* may read me your "Giants" on and on or your poems of the countryside, that rank next to immortal Virgil.[f]

[a] I.e. I shall be ready at that time; cf. 10.48.1.

[b] *Porrum sectivum*; cf. 10.48.9.

[c] From Velabrum, district of Rome on the western slope of the Palatine. Cheeses were smoked there to improve their flavor; cf. 13.32.

[d] As though to say: "But never mind the menu (you can see the style); let's pretend it will be sumptious."

[e] See 7.67.12n.

[f] I.e. the *Georgics*.

53

Claudia caeruleis cum sit Rufina Britannis
    edita, quam Latiae pectora gentis habet!
quale decus formae! Romanam credere matres
    Italides possunt, Atthides esse suam.
5 di bene quod sancto peperit fecunda marito,
    quod sperat generos quodque puella nurus.
sic placeat superis, ut coniuge gaudeat uno
    et semper natis gaudeat illa tribus.

54

Unguenta et casias et olentem funera murram
    turaque de medio semicremata rogo
et quae de Stygio rapuisti cinnama lecto,
    improbe, de turpi, Zoile, redde sinu.
5 a pedibus didicere manus peccare protervae.
    non miror furem, qui fugitivus eras.

55

Hortatur fieri quod te Lupus, Urbice, patrem,
    ne credas; nihil est quod minus ille velit.
ars est captandi quod nolis velle videri;
    ne facias optat quod rogat ut facias.

53

Though Claudia Rufina sprang from the blue[a] Britons, how Latin is her mind! What beauty of form! Italian mothers might believe her Roman, Attic mothers their own. Thank the gods, she has been fertile of offspring to her virtuous husband, and, though but a girl, hopes for sons- and daughters-in-law. So may it please the High Ones that she rejoice in one partner and rejoice always in three children.

54

Shameless Zoilus, return from your filthy pocket the unguents and the casia and the myrrh, redolent of funerals, and the half-cremated frankincense you took from the midst of the pyre, and the cinnamon you snatched from the Stygian couch. Your impudent hands learned wickedness from your feet. I don't wonder you're a thief, seeing that you used to be a runaway.

55

Lupus urges you to have children, Urbicus, but don't believe him. There's nothing he would like less. It's the art of legacy-hunting to seem to want what you don't want. He prays you won't do what he asks you

[a] Painted with woad.

5   dicat praegnantem tua se Cosconia tantum:
      pallidior fiet iam pariente Lupus.
   at tu consilio videaris ut usus amici,
      sic morere ut factum te putet esse patrem.

56

Quod nimium mortem, Chaeremon Stoice, laudas,
      vis animum mirer suspiciamque tuum?
hanc tibi virtutem fracta facit urceus ansa,
      et tristis nullo qui tepet igne focus,
5   et teges et cimex et nudi sponda grabati,
      et brevis atque eadem nocte dieque toga.
o quam magnus homo es, qui faece rubentis aceti
      et stipula et nigro pane carere potes!
Leuconicis agedum tumeat tibi culcita lanis
10   constringatque tuos purpura pexa toros,
dormiat et tecum modo qui, dum Caecuba miscet,
      convivas roseo torserat ore puer:
o quam tu cupies ter vivere Nestoris annos
      et nihil ex ulla perdere luce voles!
15   rebus in angustis facile est contemnere vitam:
      fortiter ille facit qui miser esse potest.

57

Miraris docto quod carmina mitto, Severe,
      ad cenam cum te, docte Severe, vocem?
Iuppiter ambrosia satur est et nectare vivit;
      nos tamen exta Iovi cruda merumque damus.

56.11 modo qui dum *Gronovius* : qui cum m- $\beta\gamma$ 57.1
severe γ, *SB*[1] (S-), *cf. SB*[3] : seuero β

to do. Let your Cosconia only say she's pregnant, Lupus will turn paler than a woman already in labor. But to give the appearance of having taken a friend's advice, die in such a way that he thinks you *have* a child.[a]

56

Stoic Chaeremon, because you laud death overmuch, do you wish me to admire and look up to your courage? A jug with a broken handle makes this valor of yours, and a dismal hearth unwarmed by any fire, and a mat, and a gnat, and the frame of a bare truckle bed, and a short gown worn night and day alike. What a hero you are, who can do without dregs of red vinegar and straw and black bread! Come, let your pillow swell with Leuconian wool,[b] and silky purple drape your couches, and a boy sleep with you who lately tormented the guests with his rosy face as he mixed the Caecuban: oh, how eager you will be to live three time the years of Nestor, how you will want to lose no instant of any day! It is easy to hold life cheap with straightened means: he who can be wretched plays the man.

57

Are you surprised, Severus, that I send verses to a poet when I invite you, poet Severus, to dinner? Jupiter has his fill of ambrosia and lives on nectar; yet we give raw entrails and wine to Jove. Since all

[a] I.e. leave him nothing.   [b] Cf. 14.159.

5   omnia cum tibi sint dono concessa deorum,
     si quod habes non vis, ergo quid accipies?

58

Cum me velle vides tentumque, Telesphore, sentis,
    magna rogas — puta me velle negare: licet? —
et nisi iuratus dixi 'dabo', subtrahis illas,
    permittunt in me quae tibi multa, natis.
5   quid si me tonsor, cum stricta novacula supra est,
    tunc libertatem divitiasque roget?
promittam; neque enim rogat illo tempore tonsor,
    latro rogat; res est imperiosa timor:
sed fuerit curva cum tuta novacula theca,
10   frangam tonsori crura manusque simul.
at tibi nil faciam, sed lota mentula lana
    λαικάζειν cupidae dicet avaritiae.

59

Senos Charinus omnibus digitis gerit
   nec nocte ponit anulos
nec cum lavatur. causa quae sit quaeritis?
   dactyliothecam non habet.

---

[a] Undyed wool was either "washed" (*lota*) or "greasy" (*sucida*); cf. Housman, 1182f, where the couplet is explained (in Latin).

things have been granted you by the gods' gift, if you don't want what you already have, what then will you accept?

58

When you see that I want it, Telesphorus, that I'm taut, you make large demands. Suppose I want to refuse, can I? And unless I say under oath "I'll give it," you withdraw those buttocks that let you take many liberties with me. What if my barber, with razor drawn above my throat, were to ask for freedom and wealth? I would promise, for he is not a barber, asking at such a time, but a bandit; fear is a peremptory thing. But once the razor is safely in its curved case, I shall break that barber's legs and hands together. To you, however, I shall do nothing, but with washed wool[a] my cock shall tell your eager avarice to go suck.

59

Charinus wears six rings on each finger and does not take them off at night nor when he has his bath. Do you ask the reason? He doesn't have a ring case.[b]

[b] The point seems to lie simply in the unexpectedness of the reason, unless it is implied that the rings were worthless or borrowed.

60

Sit Phlogis an Chione Veneri magis apta requiris?
    pulchrior est Chione; sed Phlogis ulcus habet;
ulcus habet Priami quod tendere possit alutam
    quodque senem Pelian non sinat esse senem;
5 ulcus habet quod habere suam vult quisque puellam,
    quod sanare Criton, non quod Hygia potest.
at Chione non sentit opus nec vocibus ullis
    adiuvat; absentem marmoreamve putes.
exorare, dei, si vos tam magna liceret
10   et bona velletis tam pretiosa dare,
hoc quod habet Chione corpus faceretis haberet
    ut Phlogis, et Chione quod Phlogis ulcus habet.

61

Lingua maritus, moechus ore Nanneius,
Summemmianis inquinatior buccis,
quem cum fenestra vidit a Suburana
obscena nudum Leda, fornicem cludit
5 mediumque mavult basiare quam summum,
modo qui per omnes viscerum tubos ibat

60

You want to know whether Phlogis or Chione[a] is the
more apt for love-making? Chione is the more beau-
tiful, but Phlogis has an itch. She has an itch that
could tauten Priam's limp strap, that would not let
old Pelias be old. She has the itch that every man
wants his girl to have, one that Criton can cure but
not Hygia.[b] But Chione does not feel what goes on or
make a sound to help, you would think she wasn't
there or made of marble. Ye gods, if it were permit-
ted to win from you so great a petition and you were
minded to grant boons so precious, you would make
Phlogis have the body that Chione has and Chione
the itch that Phlogis has.

61

Husband with his tongue, adulterer with his
mouth,[c] Nanneius is dirtier than Summemmian
lips. When foul Leda sees him naked from a window
in Subura, she closes the brothel, and she prefers
to kiss his middle rather than his top. Well, he
that lately used to go through all the inner tubes

---

[a] "Fiery" and "snowy."

[b] "Criton" purports to be a male doctor, "Hygia"
("Health," or the goddess thereof) a female doctor; cf.
11.71.7.

[c] Committing adultery with his own wife (SB^3, 134); cf.
3.84n.

et voce certa consciaque dicebat
puer an puella matris esset in ventre,
— gaudete cunni; vestra namque res acta est —
10 arrigere linguam non potest fututricem.
nam dum tumenti mersus haeret in vulva
et vagientes intus audit infantes,
partem gulosam solvit indecens morbus.
nec purus esse nunc potest nec impurus.

62

Lesbia se iurat gratis numquam esse fututam.
verum est. cum futui vult, numerare solet.

63

Spectas nos, Philomuse, cum lavamur,
et quare mihi tam mutuniati
sint leves pueri subinde quaeris.
dicam simpliciter tibi roganti:
5 pedicant, Philomuse, curiosos.

64

Nescio tam multis quid scribas, Fauste, puellis:
hoc scio, quod scribit nulla puella tibi.

and declare confidently as of personal knowledge whether boy or girl was in a mother's belly (rejoice, cunts; this is your advantage) cannot raise his fornicating tongue. For while he was stuck deep in a swelling womb and heard the infants wailing inside, an uncomely disease relaxed the greedy member. Now he can't be either clean or unclean.

62

Lesbia swears that she has never been fucked free of charge. It's true. When she wants to be fucked, she is accustomed to pay cash.

63

You watch me in the bath, Philomusus, and ask from time to time why my smooth boys are so well endowed. I'll answer your question frankly: they sodomize Nosy Parkers, Philomusus.

64

Faustus, I don't know what you write to so many girls. This much I do know, that no girl writes to you.[a]

[a] Alternative meanings: "This I know which no girl writes to you," i.e. your filthy habits; or "I know what it is that no girl writes to you," i.e. that she will do as you ask.

65

Sescenti cenant a te, Iustine, vocati
   lucis ad officium quae tibi prima fuit.
inter quos, memini, non ultimus esse solebam;
   nec locus hic nobis invidiosus erat.

   *   *   *   *   *   *   *

5 postera sed festae reddis sollemnia mensae:
   sescentis hodie, cras mihi natus eris.

66

Et delator es et calumniator,
et fraudator es et negotiator,
et fellator es et lanista. miror
quare non habeas, Vacerra, nummos.

67

Nil mihi das vivus; dicis post fata daturum.
   si non es stultus, scis, Maro, quid cupiam.

68

Parva rogas magnos; sed non dant haec quoque magni.
   ut pudeat levius, tu, Matho, magna roga.

65.4 *lac. stat.* SB[3]

65

A multitude, Justinus, dine at your invitation to celebrate the day your life began. Among them, I remember, I used not to be the last, and this place was not begrudged me . . . [a] But you are repeating the ceremony of the festive board tomorrow. For the multitude you will be born today, tomorrow for me.[b]

66

You are an informer and a slanderer, a swindler and a dealer, a sucker and a trainer.[c] I wonder why you don't have any money, Vacerra.

67

You give me nothing in your lifetime. You say you will give me something after your death. If you're not a fool, you know what I want, Maro.[d]

68

You ask small favors of big men; even these the big men refuse. To lighten your humiliation, Matho, ask big favors.[e]

[a] A couplet must have dropped out, to the effect that M. had not been invited this year.

[b] I.e. "today you will be 'not born,' so far as I am concerned"; cf. 4.83.4n.

[c] Of gladiators.

[d] Your death; cf. 8.27.

[e] Cf. 6.10.4.

69

Amphitheatrales inter nutrita magistros
    venatrix, silvis aspera, blanda domi,
Lydia dicebar, domino fidissima Dextro,
    qui non Erigones mallet habere canem,
5 nec qui Dictaea Cephalum de gente secutus
    luciferae pariter venit ad astra deae.
non me longa dies nec inutilis abstulit aetas,
    qualia Dulichio fata fuere cani:
fulmineo spumantis apri sum dente perempta,
10   quantus erat, Calydon, aut, Erymanthe, tuus.
nec queror infernas quamvis cito rapta sub umbras.
    non potui fato nobiliore mori.

70

Vendere, Tucca, potes centenis milibus emptos?
    plorantis dominos vendere, Tucca, potes?
nec te blanditiae, nec verba rudesve querelae,
    nec te dente tuo saucia colla movent?
5 ah facinus! tunica patet inguen utrimque levata,
    inspiciturque tua mentula facta manu.
si te delectat numerata pecunia, vende
    argentum, mensas, murrina, rura, domum;

---

[a] Laelaps, given to Procris by Diana and by her to her
husband Cephalus. When Cephalus was added to the
stars by Aurora, his hound followed him.

69

Reared among the trainers of the Amphitheater, a
huntress, fierce in the woods, gentle in the house, I
was called Lydia, most faithful to my master
Dexter, who would not have preferred Erigone's dog
or him of Dicte's breed[a] that followed Cephalus and
came with him to the stars of the light-bringing god-
dess. It was not length of days nor useless age that
carried me off, as was the fate of the Dulichian dog.[b]
I was slain by the lightning tusk of a foaming boar,
as huge as him of Calydon or him of Erymanthus.
Nor do I complain, though snatched untimely to the
nether shades. I could not die by a nobler fate.

70

Tucca, have you the heart to sell those you bought
for a hundred thousand apiece? Can you sell your
weeping "masters,"[c] Tucca? Do not their blandish-
ments, their words and artless plaints move you,
and their necks wounded by your tooth? Ah vil-
lainy! Their tunics are lifted on either side, their
groins revealed, and their cocks, formed by your
hand,[d] inspected. If cash down is your pleasure, sell
silver, tables, murrines, farms, town house; sell old

[b] Argus, the hound of Ulysses, that recognised him
after twenty years, and died: Hom. *Od.* 17.291–327.

[c] Cf. 5.57n.

[d] Cf. 11.22.6.

vende senes servos, ignoscent, vende paternos:
10   ne pueros vendas, omnia vende miser.
luxuria est emere hos — quis enim dubitatve negatve? —,
    sed multo maior vendere luxuria est.

71

Hystericam vetulo se dixerat esse marito
    et queritur futui Leda necesse sibi;
sed flens atque gemens tanti negat esse salutem
    seque refert potius proposuisse mori.
5 vir rogat ut vivat virides nec deserat annos,
    et fieri quod iam non facit ipse sinit.
protinus accedunt medici medicaeque recedunt,
    tollunturque pedes. o medicina gravis!

72

Drauci Natta sui vorat pipinnam,
    collatus cui gallus est Priapus.

73

Venturum iuras semper mihi, Lygde, roganti
    constituisque horam constituisque locum.
cum frustra iacui longa prurigine tentus,
    succurrit pro te saepe sinistra mihi.
5 quid precer, o fallax, meritis et moribus istis?
    umbellam luscae, Lygde, feras dominae.

72.1 vorat SB^3, *auct. Scriverio* : uocat $\beta\gamma$

slaves, they will forgive you, sell your father's slaves; sell everything, you wretch, so you don't sell the boys. Buying them is self-indulgence (who doubts or denies it?), but selling them is self-indulgence far greater.

71

Leda told her old husband that she was hysterical and complains that being fucked is a necessity for her; but with tears and moans she declares that life is not worth the price and says that she has chosen to die instead. Her man begs her to live and not forsake the years of her prime; what he does not any more do himself he allows to be done. Straight away the men doctors approach and the women doctors retire; her feet are hoisted. Drastic therapy!

72

Natta devours the willy of his young athlete, compared to whom Priapus is a eunuch.

73

When I ask you, Lygdus, you always swear that you'll come to me and you appoint a time and appoint a place. But when I have lain taut with protracted excitement in vain, often my left hand comes to my rescue in your stead. What should I wish upon you, false lad, for such deserts and such morals? Lygdus, may you carry a one-eyed mistress' sunshade.

74

Curandum penem commisit Baccara Raetus
  rivali medico. Baccara Gallus erit.

75

Theca tectus ahenea lavatur
tecum, Caelia, servus; ut quid, oro,
non sit cum citharoedus aut choraules?
non vis, ut puto, mentulam videre.
5 quare cum populo lavaris ergo?
omnes an tibi nos sumus spadones?
ergo, ne videaris invidere,
servo, Caelia, fibulam remitte.

76

Solvere, Paete, decem tibi me sestertia cogis,
  perdiderit quoniam Bucco ducenta tibi.
ne noceant, oro, mihi non mea crimina: tu qui
  bis centena potes perdere, perde decem.

77

In omnibus Vacerra quod conclavibus
consumit horas et die toto sedet,
cenaturit Vacerra, non cacaturit.

74.1 Raetus *Schneidewin* : graecus β : uetus γ

74

Baccara the Rhaetian committed his penis for treatment to a rival doctor. Baccara will be a Gaul.[a]

75

Your slave goes into the bath with you, Caelia, covered with a brass sheath; to what purpose, pray, since he is not a singer to the lyre or flute?[b] I suppose you don't want to see his cock. Then why do you bathe in public? Are we all eunuchs in your eyes? So, to avoid appearing to grudge us, unfasten your slave's sheath, Caelia.

76

You force me to pay you ten thousand sesterces, Paetus, because Bucco has lost you two hundred thousand. Please don't make me suffer for sins I have not committed. You can lose two hundred thousand; lose ten.

77

Vacerra spends hours in all the privies, sitting all day long. Vacerra doesn't want a shit, he wants a dinner.[c]

[a] I.e. a eunuch. See 2.45n.
[b] Infibulation was supposed to protect the voice; cf. 7.82.1; 14.215.
[c] He hopes to meet some acquaintance and to get an invitation.

78

Utere femineis complexibus, utere, Victor,
    ignotumque sibi mentula discat opus.
flammea texuntur sponsae, iam virgo paratur,
    tondebit pueros iam nova nupta tuos.
5 pedicare semel cupido dabit illa marito,
    dum metuit teli vulnera prima novi:
saepius hoc fieri nutrix naterque vetabunt
    et dicent: 'uxor, non puer, ista tibi est.'
heu quantos aestus, quantos patiere labores,
10   si fuerit cunnus res peregrina tibi!
ergo Suburanae tironem trade magistrae.
    illa virum faciet; non bene virgo docet.

79

Ad primum decima lapidem quod venimus hora,
    arguimur lentae crimine pigritiae.
non est ista viae, non est mea, sed tua culpa est,
    misisti mulas qui mihi, Paete, tuas.

80

Litus beatae Veneris aureum Baias,
Baias superbae blanda dona Naturae,
ut mille laudem, Flacce, versibus Baias,
laudabo digne non satis tamen Baias.
5 sed Martialem malo, Flacce, quam Baias.

78

Practice feminine embraces, Victor, do, and let your
cock learn a trade unknown to it. The veils are a-
weaving for your fiancée, the girl is already being
dressed, soon the newly-wed will be cropping your
boys. She will let her eager spouse sodomize her
once, while she fears the first wound of the new
lance, but her nurse and her mother will forbid its
happening often and say: "She's your wife, not your
boy." Ah what embarrassments, what ordeals you
will suffer if a cunt is something foreign to you!
Therefore hand yourself over as a novice to an
instructress in Subura. She will make a man of you.
A virgin is a poor teacher.

79

Because I reached the first milestone at the tenth
hour,[a] I stand accused as a lazy slowcoach. It is not
the road's fault, it is not my fault, it is yours, Paetus,
for sending me your mules.

80

Baiae, golden shore of happy Venus, Baiae, proud
nature's beguiling gift, though I praise Baiae in a
thousand verses, Flaccus, I shall never praise Baiae
as Baiae deserves. But, Flaccus, I want Martialis

[a] M. has arrived an hour late for dinner: cf. 4.8.6.

optare utrumque pariter improbi votum est.
quod si deorum munere hoc mihi detur,
quid gaudiorum est Martialis et Baiae!

81

Cum sene communem vexat spado Dindymus Aeglen
    et iacet in medio sicca puella toro.
viribus hic, operi non est hic utilis annis:
    ergo sine effectu prurit utrique labor.
5 supplex illa rogat pro se miserisque duobus,
    hunc iuvenem facias, hunc, Cytherea, virum.

82

A Sinuessanis conviva Philostratus undis
    conductum repetens nocte iubente larem
paene imitatus obît saevis Elpenora fatis,
    praeceps per longos dum ruit usque gradus.
5 non esset, Nymphae, tam magna pericula passus,
    si potius vestras ille bibisset aquas.

80.7 mihi *Gilbert* : tibi βγ

more than Baiae.[a] To ask for both together would be a presumptious prayer. Yet if this were granted me by a gift of the gods, what bliss—Martialis and Baiae!

81

Eunuch Dindymus and an old man harass Aegle in common, and the girl lies dry in the middle of the bed. Lack of strength makes the one, length of years the other useless for the job; so each labors in fruitless desire. She begs in supplication for herself and the two unfortunates, Cytherea, that you make one of them young and the other a man.

82

As Philostratus was returning at night's behest from a dinner party at the baths of Sinuessa to his rented lodging, he almost copied Elpenor and lost his life by a cruel fate, plunging down a long flight of steps. Nymphs, he would not have endured so great a peril if he had drunk your waters instead.[b]

[a] Julius Martialis. M. seems to be replying to an invitation from Flaccus and suggesting that his friend should be invited as well.
[b] Cf. 11.7.12. "Philostratus" should have drunk them instead of wine.

83

Nemo habitat gratis nisi dives et orbus apud te.
nemo domum pluris, Sosibiane, locat.

84

Qui nondum Stygias descendere quaerit ad umbras
    tonsorem fugiat, si sapit, Antiochum.
alba minus saevis lacerantur bracchia cultris,
    cum furit ad Phrygios enthea turba modos;
5 mitior implicitas Alcon secat enterocelas
    fractaque fabrili dedolat ossa manu.
tondeat hic inopes Cynicos et Stoica menta
    collaque pulverea nudet equina iuba.
hic miserum Scythica sub rupe Promethea radat,
10   carnificem nudo pectore poscet avem;
ad matrem fugiet Pentheus, ad Maenadas Orpheus,
    Antiochi tantum barbara tela sonent.
haec quaecumque meo numeratis stigmata mento,
    in vetuli pyctae qualia fronte sedent,
15 non iracundis fecit gravis unguibus uxor:
    Antiochi ferrum est et scelerata manus.
unus de cunctis animalibus hircus habet cor:
    barbatus vivit, ne ferat Antiochum.

84.10 nudo $\beta\gamma$: duro T

83

Nobody lives in your house free of charge unless he is rich and childless. Nobody, Sosibianus, lets his house at a higher rent.[a]

84

Whoever does not want to go down to the Stygian shades just yet, let him, if he is wise, shun Antiochus the barber. With knives less cruel white arms are lacerated when the frenzied throng[b] raves to the sound of Phrygian music. Alcon is more gentle when he cuts entangled hernias or hews broken bones with his carpenter's hand. Let Antiochus clip pauper Cynics and Stoic chins, let him strip horses' necks bare of their dusty manes. Were he to shave poor Prometheus under his Scythian crag, Prometheus with naked breast would call for the torturer bird. Pentheus would flee to his mother, Orpheus to the Maenads, should they so much as hear the sound of Antiochus' barbarous weapons. These scars that you count on my chin, like those that sit on the face of an elderly bruiser, none of them were made by a tyrannical wife with angry nails: it's Antiochus' steel and bloody hand. Of all animals only the billy goat has sense: he lives with a beard lest he suffer Antiochus.

[a] The rich lodgers will leave him their money.
[b] The votaries of Cybele.

85

Sidere percussa est subito tibi, Zoile, lingua,
dum lingis. certe, Zoile, nunc futuis.

86

Leniat ut fauces medicus, quas aspera vexat
assidue tussis, Parthenopaee, tibi,
mella dari nucleosque iubet dulcesque placentas
et quidquid pueros non sinit esse truces.
5   at tu non cessas totis tussire diebus.
non est haec tussis, Parthenopaee, gula est.

87

Dives eras quondam: sed tunc pedico fuisti
et tibi nulla diu femina nota fuit.
nunc sectaris anus. o quantum cogit egestas!
illa fututorem te, Charideme, facit.

88

Multis iam, Lupe, posse se diebus
pedicare negat Carisianus.
causam cum modo quaererent sodales,
ventrem dixit habere se solutum.

85.2 futuis β : -ues γ   87.2 nota β : nata γ   88.2
Carisianus] *vide ad* 6.24.1

85

Zoilus, your tongue was struck with a sudden paralysis[a] while you were licking. Surely, Zoilus, you fornicate now.

86

To soothe your throat, Parthenopaeus,[b] constantly racked by a harsh cough, the doctor orders you honey and nuts and sweet cakes and whatever keeps boys from being fractious. But you go on coughing all and every day. This is no cough, Parthenopaeus, it's greed.

87

Once you were rich, but then you were a sodomite and for a long time no woman was known to you. Now you run after crones. The things poverty makes men do! Poverty, Charidemus, makes you a fornicator.

88

Carisianus says that for many days now, Lupus, he hasn't been able to sodomize. The other day, when his friends asked him the reason, he said he had diarrhea.[c]

[a] Lit. "by a star." Cf. 7.92.9n.
[b] I.e. a handsome youth; see Index and Appendix B.
[c] Thus betraying the fact that he was a pathic.

MARTIAL

89

Intactas quare mittis mihi, Polla, coronas?
   a te vexatas malo tenere rosas.

90

Carmina nulla probas molli quae limite currunt,
   sed quae per salebras altaque saxa cadunt,
et tibi Maeonio quoque carmine maius habetur,
   'Lucili columella hic situ' Metrophanes';
5 attonitusque legis 'terrai frugiferai',
   Accius et quidquid Pacuviusque vomunt.
vis imiter veteres, Chrestille, tuosque poetas?
   dispeream ni scis mentula quid sapiat.

91

Aeolidos Canace iacet hoc tumulata sepulchro,
   ultima cui parvae septima venit hiems.
'ah scelus, ah facinus!' properas qui flere, viator,
   non licet hic vitae de brevitate queri:
5 tristius est leto leti genus: horrida vultus
   abstulit et tenero sedit in ore lues,
ipsaque crudeles ederunt oscula morbi
   nec data sunt nigris tota labella rogis.

90.3 quoque carmine maius *Lachmann* : res (quod γ) c-
maior βγ   4 situ' *Scriverius* : situ(s) est γ : situs
γ   91.3 ah . . . facinus *viatori tribui*

---

[a] From Lucilius. The uncouth elision and the suppres-
sion of final s mark the line as archaic.
[b] From Ennius, with archaic genitive endings.

74

89

Why do you send me untouched garlands, Polla? I would rather hold roses you have tumbled.

90

You do not approve of any poems that run on a smooth path, only of those that stumble among ruts and boulders; greater to you even than Maeonian song is "little pillar of Lucilius, here lieth Metrophanes."[a] In rapt amazement you read "of fruitful earth,"[b] and whatever Accius and Pacuvius spew out. Do you wish me to imitate the old poets, your poets, Chrestillus? Damned if you don't know the taste of a cock![c]

91

Aeolis' daughter Canace[d] lies buried in this tomb, a little girl to whom a seventh winter came as her last. "What a crime, what a villainy!" Traveller hastening to weep, you must not here complain of life's short span. Sadder than her death is the manner of her death. A hideous corruption stole her face and settled on her tender mouth, a cruel disease ate her very kisses and mutilated her lips before they were given to the black pyre. If fate had

[c] Double meaning: (a) You appreciate a virile style. (b) You are a fellator (see Housman, 732).

[d] Since her mother's name was Aeolis, the girl was called after the daughter of the wind god, Aeolus. As she was slave-born, her father, whether known or not, is out of the picture.

si tam praecipiti fuerant ventura volatu,
10   debuerant alia fata venire via.
sed mors vocis iter properavit cludere blandae,
     ne posset duras flectere lingua deas.

92

Mentitur qui te vitiosum, Zoile, dicit.
     non vitiosus homo es, Zoile, sed vitium.

93

Pierios vatis Theodori flamma penates
     abstulit. hoc Musis et tibi, Phoebe, placet?
o scelus, o magnum facinus crimenque deorum,
     non arsit pariter quod domus et dominus!

94

Quod nimium lives nostris et ubique libellis
     detrahis, ignosco: verpe poeta, sapis.
hoc quoque non curo, quod cum mea carmina carpas,
     compilas: et sic, verpe poeta, sapis.
5 illud me cruciat, Solymis quod natus in ipsis
     pedicas puerum, verpe poeta, meum.
ecce negas iurasque mihi per templa Tonantis.
     non credo: iura, verpe, per Anchialum.

---

[a] M. ironically admits that his poems are of no account; cf. 1.117.18; 11.106.4.

[b] This has caused an incredible amount of fantastic guesswork down the centuries, although Calderini had seen in the fifteenth that the reference is to Anchialus (or Anchiale) in Cilicia, a town founded by Sardanapalus and containing his tomb with its famous epitaph (Cic. *Tusc.*

to come in so precipitate a flight, it should have come by a different path. But death hurried to close the channel of her sweet voice, lest her tongue should prevail to sway the pitiless goddesses.

92

He lies, Zoilus, who says you are vicious. You are not a vicious man, Zoilus, you're vice.

93

Fire has consumed the Pierian home of poet Theodorus. Does this please the Muses and you, Phoebus? Oh crime, oh monstrous villainy and reproach to heaven!—that house and householder did not perish together.

94

That you are green with jealousy and run down my little books wherever you go, I forgive: circumcised poet, you show your sense.[a] This too leaves me indifferent, that you plunder my poems while you carp at them: circumcised poet, herein also you show your sense. What does upset me is that born in Jerusalem itself you sodomize my boy, circumcised poet. So! You deny it, you swear to me by the temple of the Thunderer. I don't believe you. Swear, circumcised one, by Anchialus.[b]

5.101). The libertine from Jerusalem is told that he should be swearing, not by Jupiter's temple on the Capitol (note that M. does not say "by Jupiter"), but by the oriental city where the proverbial type of sensuality (cf. 11.11.6) lay buried (SB[1]; cf. SB[3]).

95

Incideris quotiens in basia fellatorum,
    in †solium† puta te mergere, Flacce, caput.

96

Marcia, non Rhenus, salit hic, Germane: quid obstas
    et puerum prohibes divitis imbre lacus?
barbare, non debet, summoto cive ministro,
    captivam victrix unda levare sitim.

97

Una nocte quater possum: sed quattuor annis
    si possum, peream, te, Telesilla, semel.

98

Effugere non est, Flacce, basiatores.
instant, morantur, persecuntur, occurrunt
et hinc et illinc, usquequaque, quacumque.
non ulcus acre pusulaeve lucentes,
5   nec triste mentum sordidique lichenes,
nec labra pingui delibuta cerato,
nec congelati gutta proderit nasi.
et aestuantem basiant et algentem,

96.3 *post* cive *conma sustuli*

---

[a] See Appendix A.
[b] A pool with fountains fed by the Marcian aqueduct is
indicated; cf. 9.18.6.

95

Whenever you encounter suckers' kisses, just imagine, Flaccus, that you are plunging your head into a closestool.[a]

96

Marcia[b] leaps here, German, not the Rhine. Why do you stand in the way and keep the boy from the rain of the generous pool? Barbarian, it is not fitting that victorious water should relieve captive thirst and a citizen servant[c] be elbowed aside.

97

I can manage it four times in a night. But confound me if I can manage you, Telesilla, once in four years.

98

Flaccus, one just can't escape kissers.[d] They press, they stay, they pursue, they encounter, from this side and from that, anywhere, everywhere. An active ulcer, bright blisters, a diseased chin,[e] dirty scabs, lips smeared thick with oily wax-salve, drop from a frozen nose—none of these will avail. They kiss you when you're sweltering and when you're

[c] Both are slaves, but the native is facetiously called a citizen by contrast with the barbarian.

[d] See on the same subject 7.95 and 12.59.

[e] An allusion to the *mentagra*, a skin disease attacking first the chin, and propagated by kissing: cf. Pliny *N.H.* 26.2.

et nuptiale basium reservantem.
10 non te cucullis asseret caput tectum,
lectica nec te tuta pelle veloque,
nec vindicabit sella saepibus clusa:
rimas per omnis basiator intrabit.
non consulatus ipse, non tribunatus
15 senive fasces nec superba clamosi
lictoris abiget virga basiatorem:
sedeas in alto tu licet tribunali
et e curuli iura gentibus reddas,
ascendet illa basiator atque illa.
20 febricitantem basiabit et flentem,
dabit oscitanti basium natantique,
dabit cacanti. remedium mali solum est,
facias amicum basiare quem nolis.

99

De cathedra quotiens surgis — iam saepe notavi —
pedicant miserae, Lesbia, te tunicae.
quas cum conata es dextra, conata sinistra
vellere, cum lacrimis eximis et gemitu:
5 sic constringuntur gemina Symplegade culi,
ut nimias intrant Cyaneasque natis.
emendare cupis vitium deforme? docebo:
Lesbia, nec surgas censeo nec sedeas.

98.12 saepibus *Walter* : -ius βγ   22 dabit β : -t et γ
23 nolis γ : non uis β   99.5 gemina γ : magni (-is T)
Tβ   6 ut *scripsi* : et Tβγ

shivering and when you're keeping a kiss for your bride. A cowled head won't set you free, nor a litter screened by skin and curtain, nor will a chair shut in by barriers protect you; the kisser will enter through every chink. Not the consulship itself, nor the tribunate or the six *fasces*,[a] nor the haughty rod of the bawling lictor will drive off the kisser. Though you sit on a high tribunal and from curule chair give judgment to nations, the kisser will climb up one way or another. He will kiss you when you are in fever and in tears, yawning and swimming— and shitting. The only remedy for the plague is to make a friend of someone you would not wish to kiss.[b]

99

Whenever you get up from your chair (I have noticed it again and again), your unfortunate tunic sodomizes you, Lesbia. You try and try to pluck it with your left hand and your right, till you extract it with tears and groans. So firmly is it constrained by the twin Symplegades of your arse as it enters your oversized, Cyanean buttocks. Do you want to correct this ugly fault? I'll tell you how. Lesbia, I advise you neither to get up nor sit down.

[a] The six lictors carrying rods and axes in attendance on a praetor.
[b] That is: Let Flaccus make friends with a *fellator*. As a favor to Flaccus the *fellator* will kiss anyone who kisses him (Flaccus). The *basiatores* will then leave Flaccus alone (*SB³*; cf. *SB¹*).

100

Habere amicam nolo, Flacce, subtilem,
cuius lacertos anuli mei cingant
quae clune nudo radat et genu pungat,
cui serra lumbis, cuspis eminet culo.
5   sed idem amicam nolo mille librarum.
carnarius sum, pinguiarius non sum.

101

Thaida tam tenuem potuisti, Flacce, videre?
   tu, puto, quod non est, Flacce, videre potes.

102

Non est mentitus qui te mihi dixit habere
   formosam carnem, Lydia, non faciem.
est ita, si taceas et si tam muta recumbas
   quam silet in cera vultus et in tabula.
5   sed quotiens loqueris, carnem quoque, Lydia, perdis
   et sua plus nulli quam tibi lingua nocet.
audiat aedilis ne te videatque caveto:
   portentum est, quotiens coepit imago loqui.

100

Flaccus, I don't want a slender girl friend whose
arms would be encircled by my rings, who would
shave me with her bare haunch and prick me with
her knee, who has a saw projecting from her loins
and a spearhead from her arse.[a] But neither do I
want a girl friend weighing a thousand pounds.[b] I
am a flesh-fancier, not a fat-fancier.

101

Could you see Thais, so thin as she is? I think,
Flaccus, you can see what isn't there.

102

He told me no lie, the man who told me that you
have beautiful flesh, Lydia, but not a beautiful face.
That's so, if you would keep quiet and recline as
mute as a silent countenance in wax or in a paint-
ing. But whenever you speak, you spoil your flesh
too; nobody's tongue damages its owner more than
yours does you, Lydia. Take care the aedile doesn't
hear and see you. It's a prodigy when a statue starts
to speak.[c]

[a] "The subjunctives *cingant radat pungat* are condi-
tional ... 'serra lumbis eminet' is absolute" Housman,
1103.

[b] About 750 lbs avoirdupois.

[c] It was the duty of the aedile to report all prodigies,
such as a talking statue.

103

Tanta tibi est animi probitas orisque, Safroni,
    ut mirer fieri te potuisse patrem.

104

Uxor, vade foras aut moribus utere nostris:
    non sum ego nec Curius nec Numa nec Tatius.
me iucunda iuvant tractae per pocula noctes:
    tu properas pota surgere tristis aqua.
5 tu tenebris gaudes: me ludere teste lucerna
    et iuvat admissa rumpere luce latus.
fascia te tunicaeque obscuraque pallia celant:
    at mihi nulla satis nuda puella iacet.
basia me capiunt blandas imitata columbas:
10   tu mihi das aviae qualia mane soles.
nec motu dignaris opus nec voce iuvare
    nec digitis, tamquam tura merumque pares:
masturbabantur Phrygii post ostia servi,
    Hectoreo quotiens sederat uxor equo,
15 et quamvis Ithaco stertente pudica solebat
    illic Penelope semper habere manum.
pedicare negas: dabat hoc Cornelia Graccho,
    Iulia Pompeio, Porcia, Brute, tibi;
dulcia Darbanio nondum miscente ministro
20   pocula Iuno fuit pro Ganymede Iovi.
si te delectat gravitas, Lucretia toto
    sis licet usque die: Laida nocte volo.

---

[a] For ritual purposes. At such a time chastity would be
required.

BOOK XI

103

Your modesty of mind and appearance is such,
Safronius, that I wonder you could make a father.

104

Wife, get out of my house or conform to my ways. I
am no Curius or Numa or Tatius. I like nights
drawn out by cups that cheer: you drink water and
hasten sour-faced from the table. You love the dark:
I prefer to sport with a lamp for witness and to
admit the daylight when I'm bursting my loins. You
hide yourself with a brassiere and a tunic and an
obscuring robe: but no girl lies naked enough for me.
I am captivated by kisses that copy blandishing
doves: you give me such as you give your grand-
mother of a morning. You don't deign to help the
business along by movement or voice or fingers, as
though you were preparing incense and wine.[a] The
Phrygian slaves used to masturbate behind the door
whenever Hector's wife sat her horse, and although
the Ithacan was snoring, chaste Penelope always
used to keep her hand *there*. You won't let me
sodomize: Cornelia used to do that favor for
Gracchus, and Julia for Pompey, and Porcia,
Brutus, for you.[b] Before the Dardanian page mixed
their sweet cups, Juno was Jupiter's Ganymede. If
grave manners please you, you may be Lucretia all
day: at night I want Lais.

[b] Doubtless an assumption on M.'s part; cf. 11.43.9.

105

Mittebas libram, quadrantem, Garrice, mittis.
   saltem semissem, Garrice, solve mihi.

106

   Vibi Maxime, si vacas havere,
   hoc tantum lege: namque et occupatus
   et non es nimium laboriosus.
   transis hos quoque quattuor? sapisti.

107

Explicitum nobis usque ad sua cornua librum
   et quasi perlectum, Septiciane, refers.
omnia legisti. credo, scio, gaudeo, verum est.
   perlegi libros sic ego quinque tuos.

108

Quamvis tam longo possis satur esse libello,
   lector, adhuc a me disticha pauca petis.
sed Lupus usuram puerique diaria poscunt.
   lector, solve. taces dissimulasque? vale.

107.4 Quinte *Heinsius*

BOOK XI

105

You used to send a pound, Garricus, now you send a quarter. At least pay me half, Garricus.[a]

106

Vibius Maximus, if you have time to say hello, read only this; for you are a busy man and not over-industrious. Do you pass by these four verses too? You show your sense.

107

You bring the book back to me unrolled to its horns[b] as though you had read it through, Septicianus. You have read everything, I believe it, I know it, I'm delighted, it's true. In the same way I read through *your* five books.

108

Reader, although you might well be satiated with so long a little book, you ask me for a few couplets more. But Lupus demands his interest and the boys their rations. Pay up, reader. You say nothing and pretend not to hear? Good-bye.

[a] Of what you "owe" me.
[b] *Cornua* are the bosses (*umbilici*) at the end of the stick round which the roll was wrapped. Cf. 4.89.2n.

LIBER XII

VALERIUS MARTIALIS PRISCO SUO SALUTEM

Scio me patrocinium debere contumacissimae
trienni desidiae; quo absolvenda non esset inter
illas quoque urbicas occupationes, quibus facilius
consequimur ut molesti potius quam ut officiosi esse
5 videamur; nedum in hac provinciali solitudine, ubi
nisi etiam intemperanter studemus, et sine solacio
et sine excusatione secessimus. accipe ergo
rationem. in qua hoc maximum et primum est, quod
civitatis aures quibus assueveram quaero, et videor
10 mihi in alieno foro litigare; si quid est enim quod in
libellis meis placeat, dictavit auditor: illam iudi-
ciorum subtilitatem, illud materiarum ingenium,
bibliothecas, theatra, convictus, in quibus studere
se voluptates non sentiunt, ad summam omnia illa
15 quae delicati reliquimus desideramus quasi desti-
tuti. accedit his municipalium robigo dentium et
iudici loco livor, et unus aut alter mali, in pusillo
loco multi; adversus quod difficile est habere cotidie

Epist. 2 quo γ : *om.* β : quae ς   4 ut β : *om.* γ
14 omnia *Friedländer* -ium βγ : *del. coni. Heraeus*

BOOK XII

VALERIUS MARTIALIS TO HIS FRIEND PRISCUS
GREETINGS

I know I am due to offer a defense of my three years'
obstinate indolence, by which defense, however, it
could not have been absolved even amid the occupa-
tions of the city, whereby we more easily manage to
appear troublesome than conscientious, much less
in this provincial solitude, where my retirement has
neither solace nor excuse unless I study to the point
of intemperance. So let me give you my reasons.
The first and most important point is that I miss the
ears of the community to which I had grown accus-
tomed. It is like pleading a case in a strange court.
For if there is anything to please in my little books,
the audience dictated it. The subtlety of judgments,
the inspiration of the themes, the libraries, the
theaters, the gatherings where pleasure is a student
without realizing it, to sum it all up, all those things
which in my fastidiousness I forsook, I now regret as
though they had deserted me. Add to this the tartar
of municipal teeth, envy in place of judgment, and
one or two malign individuals—in a tiny place a
large number. To keep a good temper every day in

bonum stomachum: ne mireris igitur abiecta ab
20 indignante quae a gestiente fieri solebant. Ne quid
tamen et advenienti tibi ab urbe et exigenti
negarem — cui non refero gratiam, si tantum ea
praesto quae possum —, imperavi mihi quod indul-
gere consueram, et studui paucissimis diebus, ut
25 familiarissimas mihi aures tuas exciperem adven-
toria sua. tu velim ista, quae tantum apud te non
periclitantur, diligenter aestimare et excutere non
graveris; et, quod tibi difficillimum est, de nugis
nostris iudices candore seposito, ne Romam, si ita
30 decreveris, non Hispaniensem librum mittamus, sed
Hispanum.

1

Retia dum cessant latratoresque Molossi
  et non invento silva quiescit apro,
otia, Prisce, brevi poteris donare libello.
  hora nec aestiva est nec tibi tota perit.

Epist. 29 candore *Housman* : nidore β : nitore γ

ᵃ The *cena adventoria* was a dinner given to one arriv-
ing from abroad. The phrase here represents a book of epi-
grams which was handed to Terentius Priscus on his
arrival in Spain in the winter of 101, and immediately for-
warded to Rome. This book, having been written *paucis-
simis diebus*, is probably the *brevis libellus* of 12.1.3 and
not Book XII as we have it, which was probably an
enlarged edition, perhaps compiled even after Martial's
death, and which certainly contains epigrams written ear-
lier than 101, e.g. 5, 8, 11, and 15. So Friedländer (Ker).

face of this is not easy. Do not be surprised there-
fore if I cast aside in disgust what I used to accom-
plish with enthusiasm. But rather than deny your
request on your arrival from Rome (for I am
ungrateful to you if I merely do for you what I can), I
have laid upon myself as a task what used to be an
indulgence and devoted a very few days to literary
effort, in order that I may receive your so familiar
ears with the dinner of welcome[a] that is their due. I
hope that you will not find it too much trouble to
appraise with care and examine these productions,
which only in your hands are in no danger, and,
what is very difficult for you, to judge my trifles
without favorable bias, lest I send to Rome (if you
so decree) a book that is not only from Spain but
Spanish.

1

While the nets and barking Molossians are idle and
no boar found and the wood reposes, you will be able
to give your leisure, Priscus, to a short volume.[b] The
hour is not summer's, and you will not lose all of it.[c]

[b] Studious men used to read or write in the intervals of
the chase: Pliny *Ep.* 1.6; 5.18.
[c] A Roman hour, being a twelfth of the time between
sunrise and sunset, was shorter in winter. And the book,
says M., will not take a whole hour to read.

2 (3)

Ad populos mitti qui nuper ab urbe solebas,
 ibis io Romam, nunc peregrine liber,
auriferi de gente Tagi tetricique Salonis,
 dat patrios amnes quos mihi terra potens.
5 non tamen hospes eris nec iam potes advena dici,
 cuius habet fratres tot domus alta Remi.
iure tuo veneranda novi pete limina templi,
 reddita Pierio sunt ubi tecta choro.
vel si malueris, prima gradiere Subura;
10 atria sunt illic consulis alta mei:
laurigeros habitat facundus Stella penatis,
 clarus Hyanteae Stella sititor aquae;
fons ibi Castalius vitreo torrente superbit,
 unde novem dominas saepe bibisse ferunt:
15 ille dabit populo patribusque equitique legendum,
 nec nimium siccis perleget ipse genis.
quid titulum poscis? versus duo tresve legantur,
 clamabunt omnes te, liber, esse meum.

2.4 amnes quos *Housman* : manes quod γ : m- quae
β   mihi γ : tibi β   8 tecta *Heinsius* (*cf. SB*[1]) : tem-
pla βγ   12 sititor γ : peti- β

---

[a] The temple of Augustus on the slope of the Palatine
facing the Capitoline had a library which Domitian seems
to have removed (perhaps because of a fire; cf. Suet. *Dom.*
20) and Trajan to have replaced. It contained M.'s earlier
works.
[b] Stella was consul A.D. 101.

2 (3)

Book that used to be sent from the City to the peoples of the world, forward, hie you to Rome, a foreigner now, from the nation of gold-bearing Tagus and rigorous Salo, ancestral rivers given me by a mighty land. But you will be no stranger, nor can you now be termed a newcomer, when the lofty house of Remus holds so many of your brethren. As of right, seek the august threshold of the New Temple,[a] where their house has been restored to the Pierian choir. Or, if you prefer, you will walk through the entrance of Sabura. There are the lofty halls of my consul;[b] eloquent Stella dwells in the laureled home, famous Stella, who thirsts for Hyantean waters.[c] Here a Castalian spring flaunts with glassy stream, from which they say the Nine Ladies have often drunk.[d] He will give you to people and Fathers and knights for them to read, and will peruse you himself with eyes not altogether dry. Why do you ask a title? Let two verses or three be read, and all men, book, will exclaim that you are mine.

[c] I.e. Boeotian, meaning the fountain Permessus on Mt Helicon (cf. 8.70.3n). The reading *Iantheae*, supposed to refer to Stella's Ianthis, was exorcized by Housman, 898f.

[d] Cf. 6.47.

3 (4)

Quod Flacco Varioque fuit summoque Maroni
    Maecenas, atavis regibus ortus eques,
gentibus et populis hoc te mihi, Prisce Terenti,
    fama fuisse loquax chartaque dicet anus.
5 tu facis ingenium, tu, si quid posse videmur;
    tu das ingenuae ius mihi pigritiae.
macte animi, quem rarus habet, morumque tuorum
    quos Numa, quos hilaris possit habere Cato.
largiri, praestare, breves extendere census
10   et dare quae faciles vix tribuere dei,
nunc licet et fas est. sed tu sub principe duro
    temporibusque malis ausus es esse bonus.

4 (5)

Longior undecimi nobis decimique libelli
    artatus labor est et breve rasit opus.
plura legant vacui, quibus otia tuta dedisti:
    haec lege tu, Caesar; forsan et illa leges.

BOOK XII

3 (4 + 6.7–12)

What Maecenas, knight sprung from ancient kings,[a]
was to Flaccus and Varius and Maro the Supreme,
this, Priscus Terentius, loquacious fame and paper
grown old shall declare to all races and peoples that
you were to me. You make my talent, any ability I
seem to show; you give me the right to a liberal idle-
ness. Bless the rare heart of you and bless your
ways, such as Numa might have or a merry Cato.
To be munificent, to provide, to increase narrow
means, and give what indulgent gods have scarce
bestowed is now allowed and lawful. But you dared
to be generous under a harsh prince and in evil
times.

4 (5)

The longer labor of my tenth and eleventh books has
been compressed and has filed[b] down my work to
brevity. Let idlers, to whom you have given leisure
in security, read more: these, Caesar, are for you to
read. Perhaps you will read those others as well.[c]

[a] Hor. *Odes* 1.1.

[b] He might have said: "I have filed."

[c] M. here presents a selection from Books X and XI. He
hopes Caesar (Nerva) will read the fuller work as well.

5 (2 + 6, 1–6)

Quae modo litoreos ibatis carmina Pyrgos,
    ite Sacra, iam non pulverulenta, via.
contigit Ausoniae procerum mitissimus aulae
    Nerva: licet tuto nunc Helicone frui:
5 recta fides, hilaris clementia, cauta potestas
    iam redeunt; longi terga dedere metus.
hoc populi gentesque tuae, pia Roma, precantur:
    dux tibi sit semper talis, et iste diu.

(6) 7

Toto vertice quot gerit capillos
annos si tot habet Ligeia, trima est.

8

Terrarum dea gentiumque Roma,
cui par est nihil et nihil secundum,
Traiani modo laeta cum futuros
tot per saecula computaret annos,
5 et fortem iuvenemque Martiumque
in tanto duce militem videret,
dixit praeside gloriosa tali:
'Parthorum procere ducesque Serum,
Thraces, Sauromatae, Getae, Britanni,
10 possum ostendere Caesarem; venite.'

5.4 tuto *tempt. Friedländer* : toto βγ

---

^a In December the road from Pyrgi to Rome would not
be dusty. But in Spain, in early autumn, when the poems

5 (2 + 6.1–6)

Poems that were lately on their way to Pyrgi by sea, go, no longer dusty, by the Sacred Way.[a] The Ausonian palace has had the good fortune to acquire the mildest of Rome's grandees, Nerva. Now we may enjoy Helicon in safety. Unswerving honor, cheerful clemency, circumspect power now return. The terrors that were with us so long have taken flight. Loyal Rome, the prayer of your peoples and nations is this: may your Leader ever be such as he, and long be he.

(6)

7

If Ligeia has as many years as she carries hairs on her entire head, she is three years old.

8

When Rome, goddess of lands and nations, that has no equal and no second, was joyfully reckoning Trajan's[b] future years through so many generations, and saw in so great a Leader a soldier, brave and young and martial, proud of such a ruler she spoke: "Nobles of Parthia and chieftains of the Seres, ye Thracians, Sarmatians, Getans, Britons, I can show you a Caesar: come."

will have begun their journey, they would find dusty roads between Bilbilis and the coast.
[b] Succeeded Nerva in January 98.

9

Palma regit nostros, mitissime Caesar, Hiberos,
  et placido fruitur Pax peregrina iugo.
ergo agimus laeti tanto pro munere grates:
  misisti mores in loca nostra tuos.

10

Habet Africanus miliens, tamen captat.
Fortuna multis dat nimis, satis nulli.

11

Parthenio dic, Musa, tuo nostroque salutem:
  nam quis ab Aonio largius amne bibit?
cuius Pipleo lyra clarior exit ab antro?
  quam plus Pierio de grege Phoebus amat?
5 et si forte — sed hoc vix est sperare — vacabit,
  tradat ut ipse duci carmina nostra roga,
quattuor et tantum timidumque brevemque libellum
  commendet verbis: 'hunc tua Roma legit.'

12

Omnia promittis cum tota nocte bibisti;
  mane nihil praestas. Pollio, mane bibe.

11.4 quam *scripsi* : quem β (*deest* γ)

---

[a] Trajan was born A.D. 52 at Italica, near Seville.
[b] The Muses.
[c] The short book was probably the abridgement of
Books X and XI mentioned in 12.4.

9

Caesar most mild, Palma governs our[a] Iberians and
Peace overseas enjoys his gentle sway. Therefore
we happily thank you for so great a boon. You have
sent your manners to our land.

10

Africanus has a hundred million, but still he fishes
for legacies. Fortune gives too much to many, to
none enough.

11

Give greetings, Muse, to your and my Parthenius.
For who drinks more largely from the Aonian
stream? Whose lyre comes forth from the Piplean
grotto with a clearer tone? Which of the Pierian
flock[b] does Phoebus love more? And if perchance
(though this can scarce be hoped for) he has time to
spare, ask him to hand my verses personally to the
Leader and commend my timid, brief little book[c]
with only four words: "This your Rome reads."

12

You promise everything when you have drunk all
night. In the morning you perform nothing. Drink
in the morning, Pollio.

13

Genus, Aucte, lucri divites habent iram:
odisse quam donare vilius constat.

14

Parcius utaris moneo rapiente veredo,
    Prisce, nec in lepores tam violentus eas.
saepe satisfecit praedae venator et acri
    decidit excussus nec rediturus equo.
5 insidias et campus habet: nec fossa nec agger
    nec sint saxa licet, fallere plana solent.
non deerit qui tanta tibi spectacula praestet,
    invidia fati sed leviore cadat.
si te delectant animosa pericula, Tuscis
10   — tutior est virtus — insidiemur apris.
quid te frena iuvant temeraria? saepius illis,
    Prisce, datum est equitem rumpere quam leporem.

15

Quidquid Parrhasia nitebat aula
donatum est oculis deisque nostris.

---

  [a] Cf. 3.37.

  [b] Priscus, like Licinianus, was a Celtiberian: cf. 1.49.-
26n.

  [c] A baffling couplet. Watching other people would not
compensate Priscus for the loss of his own sport (cf. *SB*[1];
but the solution there proposed can hardly be right).

13

Rich men, Auctus, think of anger as a sort of money-making: hating comes cheaper than giving.[a]

14

I warn you, Priscus, to use your tearaway hunter more sparingly and not to go for the hares with such violence.[b] Often has the huntsman made atonement to his quarry and been thrown off his high-mettled horse to the ground, never to remount. Even the flat is treacherous; though there be no ditch or mound or stones, level going is apt to deceive. There will not be lacking someone to provide you with such spectacles, who would fall, however, with less reproach to fate.[c] If daring hazards delight you, let us lie in ambush for Tuscan boars—a safer form of courage. Why do you love to ride recklessly? Such riding, Priscus, more often results in rupturing[d] the horseman than the hare.

15

Whatever used to shine in the Parrhasian palace has been bestowed upon our eyes and our gods.[e]

[d] Cf. 1.49.25.

[e] It appears that Nerva or Trajan had placed the treasures of Domitian's palace in temples, where the public could see them.

miratur Scythicas virentis auri
flammas Iuppiter et stupet superbi
5 regis delicias gravesque luxus:
haec sunt pocula quae decent Tonantem,
haec sunt quae Phrygium decent ministrum.
omnes cum Iove nunc sumus beati;
at nuper — pudet, ah pudet fateri —
10 omnes cum Iove pauperes eramus.

16

Addixti, Labiene, tres agellos;
emisti, Labiene, tres cinaedos:
pedicas, Labiene, tres agellos.

17

Quare tam multis a te, Laetine, diebus
non abeat febris quaeris et usque gemis.
gestatur tecum pariter pariterque lavatur;
cenat boletos, ostrea, sumen, aprum;
5 ebria Setino fit saepe et saepe Falerno,
nec nisi per niveam Caecuba potat aquam;
circumfusa rosis et nigra recumbit amomo,
dormit et in pluma purpureoque toro.
cui sit tam pulchre, quae tam bene vivat apud te,
10 ad Damam potius vis tua febris eat?

15.5 luxus *Iunius* : lusus β (*deest* γ)   17.9 cui sit tam
scripsi : cum sit ei β : cum sit tam *excerpta Parisina* (*saec.*
XIII) : cum recubet T   quae *scripsi* : cum T$\beta\gamma$

Jupiter marvels at the Scythian rays of green gold and views in amazement the whims and oppressive luxuries of a haughty monarch.[a] Here are cups that beseem the Thunderer, here cups that beseem his Phrygian page. Now we are all wealthy along with Jove; but not long ago (ah, shameful admission!) we were all poor along with Jove.

16

You put up three small fields for sale, Labienus. You bought three queens, Labienus. You sodomize three small fields, Labienus.[b]

17

You ask why your fever does not leave you after so many days, Laetinus, and groan and groan. It rides in your litter with you and bathes with you. It dines on mushrooms, oysters, udder, boar. It often gets drunk on Setine, often on Falernian, and drinks Caecuban only through snow water. It reclines wreathed in roses and black with pomade, and sleeps on feathers and a purple bed. Having such a fine time, living so well with you, would you have your fever move to Dama[c] instead?

[a] Domitian, perhaps with Tarquinius Superbus, Rome's last king, in mind.
[b] See 3.48n.
[c] I.e. a slave or poor freedman.

18

Dum tu forsitan inquietus erras
clamosa, Iuvenalis, in Subura
aut collem dominae teris Dianae;
dum per limina te potentiorum
5   sudatrix toga ventilat vagumque
maior Caelius et minor fatigant:
me multos repetita post Decembres
accepit mea rusticumque fecit
auro Bilbilis et superba ferro.
10 hic pigri colimus labore dulci
Boterdum Plateamque — Celtiberis
haec sunt nomina crassiora terris — :
ingenti fruor improboque somno
quem nec tertia saepe rumpit hora,
15 et totum mihi nunc repono quidquid
ter denos vigilaveram per annos.
ignota est toga, sed datur petenti
rupta proxima vestis a cathedra.
surgentem focus excipit superba
20 vicini strue cultus iliceti,
multa vilica quem coronat olla.
venator sequitur, sed ille quem tu
secreta cupias habere silva;
dispensat pueris rogatque longos
25 levis ponere vilicus capillos.
sic me vivere, sic iuvat perire.

18

While you perhaps, Juvenal, wander restlessly in noisy Subura or tread Lady Diana's hill,[a] while your sweating gown fans you as you cross the thresholds of the powerful and the Greater and Lesser Caelian[b] tire out the wanderer: me my Bilbilis, proud of her gold and iron, revisited after many Decembers, has received and made a rustic. Here in idleness I exert myself pleasantly to visit Boterdus and Platea (such are the uncouth names in Celtiberian lands). I enjoy an enormous, indecent amount of sleep, often unbroken till past the third hour, and pay myself back in full now for my vigils of thirty years. The gown is unknown, but when I ask I am handed the nearest garment to hand from a broken chair.[c] When I get up, a fireplace welcomes me stocked with a proud pile of logs from an adjacent oak wood and crowned by the bailiff's wife with many a pot. The huntsman comes next, but one that you would like to have with you in a secret grove. The smooth-skinned bailiff gives my boys their rations and asks me to let him cut his long hair. So fain would I live, so fain would I die.

[a] The Aventine.
[b] The Mons Caelius properly consisted of the Caelius and the Caeliolus, a lesser height.
[c] And so empty (not to be sat on).

19

In thermis sumit lactucas, ova, lacertum,
et cenare domi se negat Aemilius.

20

Quare non habeat, Fabulle, quaeris
uxorem Themison? habet sororem.

21

Municipem rigidi quis te, Marcella, Salonis
et genitam nostris quis putet esse locis?
tam rarum, tam dulce sapis. Palatia dicent,
audierint si te vel semel, esse suam;
5   nulla nec in media certabit nata Subura
nec Capitolini collis alumna tibi;
nec cito prodibit peregrini gloria partus
Romanam deceat quam magis esse nurum.
tu desiderium dominae mihi mitius urbis
10   esse iubes: Romam tu mihi sola facis.

22

Quam sit lusca Philaenis indecenter
vis dicam breviter tibi, Fabulle?
esset caeca decentior Philaenis.

21.7 prodibit SB^1 : ridebit $\beta\gamma$

19

Aemilius consumes lettuces, eggs, mackerel in the baths and says he is not dining at home.

20

Fabullus, you ask why Themison doesn't have a wife. He has[a] a sister.

21

Marcella, who would think you were a citizen of ice-cold Salo and born in these regions of ours? You have so rare, so pleasing a quality. The Palatine, if it hears you but once, will say you are its own. Nobody born in the middle of Subura, no daughter of Capitol Hill, will be your rival, nor soon will one more meet to be a Roman bride come forth as the glory of a foreign child-bed. You bid me assuage my yearning for the imperial city; you by yourself make Rome for me.

22

Do you want me to tell you in a nutshell how uncomely Philaenis is with her one eye, Fabullus? Philaenis would be more comely if she were blind.

[a] *Habet* has a secondary sense, "has sex with." But it is untrue that "sister" may also mean "mistress"; see Housman 734f.

23

Dentibus atque comis — nec te pudet — uteris emptis.
quid facies oculo, Laelia? non emitur.[a]

24

O iucunda, covinne, solitudo,
carruca magis essedoque gratum
facundi mihi munus Aeliani!
hic mecum licet, hic, Iuvate, quidquid
5 in buccam tibi venerit loquaris:
non rector Libyci niger caballi
succinctus neque cursor antecedit;
nusquam mulio: mannuli tacebunt.
o si conscius esset hic Avitus!
10 aurem non ego tertiam timerem.
totus quam bene sic dies abiret!

25

Cum rogo te nummos sine pignore, 'non habeo' inquis;
idem, si pro me spondet agellus, habes:
quod mihi non credis veteri, Telesine, sodali,
credis coliculis arboribusque meis.
5 ecce reum Carus te detulit: adsit agellus.
exilio comitem quaeris: agellus eat.

24.9 *dist. SB*[1]   25.6 exilio ς : -lii β : exilli T : exili γ

---

[a] I.e. about it. Not "for an eye." "Laelia" may be supposed to have something wrong with one of her eyes.

23

You use bought teeth and hair and are not ashamed of it. What will you do with your eye,[a] Laelia? That's not to be bought.

24

Chaise,[b] pleasant seclusion, more welcome than coach or curricle, eloquent Aelianus' gift to me! Here with me, Juvatus, here you may say whatever comes into your head. No black rider of a Libyan nag or high-girt runner goes ahead. No muleteer anywhere. The ponies will hold their tongues. If only Avitus were here to share our talk! I should not fear a third pair of ears. How nicely would a whole day pass so!

25

When I ask you for money with no security, you say: "I don't have it." But if my little farm goes surety for me, you do have it. The credit you don't give me, an old comrade, Telesinus, you give to my cabbage sprouts and trees. See now, Carus[c] has brought charges against you; let the farm appear on your behalf. You want a companion in exile: let the farm go.

[b] The *covinnus*, originally a Celtic war chariot, evidently seated at least three.

[c] I.e. an informer (delator); see Index and Appendix B.

26 (27)

A latronibus esse te fututam
dicis, Saenia: sed negant latrones.

27 (28)

Poto ego sextantes, tu potas, Cinna, deunces:
et quereris quod non, Cinna, bibamus idem?

28 (29)

Hermogenes tantus mapparum, – ◡ ◡, fur est
    quantus nummorum vix, puto, Massa fuit;
tu licet observes dextram teneasque sinistram,
    inveniet mappam qua ratione trahat:
5 cervinus gelidum sorbet sic halitus anguem,
    casuras alte sic rapit Iris aquas.
nuper cum Myrino peteretur missio laeso,
    subduxit mappas quattuor Hermogenes;
cretatam praetor cum vellet mittere mappam,
10 praetori mappam surpuit Hermogenes.

28–29 *om.* γ β

---

[a] Cf. 10.95n.

[b] Hermes was the thief among the gods: cf. Hor. *Od.*
1.10.7; accordingly M. invents the name "Sprung of
Hermes."

[c] A name, such as *Pontice*, has dropped out.

[d] Baebius Massa was found guilty of peculation in his
province of Baetica in A.D. 93. But the name may be "asso-
ciative," referring to an imaginary pickpocket.

26 (27)

You say you were fucked by bandits, Saenia; but the bandits deny it.[a]

27 (28)

I drink two measures, you, Cinna, drink eleven. And you grumble, Cinna, because we don't drink the same wine?

28 (29)

Hermogenes[b] is as mighty a thief of napkins, Ponticus(?),[c] as Massa[d] hardly was (I suppose) of money. You may watch his right hand and hold his left,[e] he will find a way to abstract a napkin. So a stag's breath sucks up a chilly snake;[f] so Iris[g] snatches water that will later fall from aloft. The other day, when the people were calling for injured Myrinus' discharge, Hermogenes sneaked four napkins.[h] When the praetor wanted to throw down

[e] The left was the thievish hand (Cat. 47.1; Ov. *Met.* 13.111); hence M.'s distinction between watching and holding.

[f] According to Pliny (*N.H.* 8.118), stags with their breath draw serpents out of their holes; cf. also Lucr. 6.765.

[g] The rainbow; cf. 4.19.10.

[h] Handkerchiefs were waved when a discharge or quarter was wished by the spectators for a gladiator: cf. Sp. 31.3.

attulerat mappam nemo, dum furta timentur:
    mantele e mensa surpuit Hermogenes.
hoc quoque si derit, medios discingere lectos
    mensarumque pedes non timet Hermogenes.
15 quamvis non modico caleant spectacula sole,
    vela reducuntur cum venit Hermogenes.
festinant trepidi substringere carbasa nautae,
    ad portum quotiens paruit Hermogenes.
linigeri fugiunt calvi sistrataque turba,
20   inter adorantes cum stetit Hermogenes.
ad cenam Hermogenes mappam non attulit umquam,
    e cena semper rettulit Hermogenes.

29 (26)

Sexagena teras cum limina mane senator,
    esse tibi videor desidiosus eques,
quod non a prima discurram luce per urbem
    et referam lassus basia mille domum.
5 sed tu, purpureis ut des nova nomina fastis
    aut Nomadum gentes Cappadocumve regas:
at mihi, quem cogis medios abrumpere somnos
    et matutinum ferre patique lutum,
quid petitur? rupta cum pes vagus exit aluta
10   et subitus crassae decidit imber aquae

28–29 *om.* γ   28.12 *et* 22 e ς : αβ   29.6 regas
Heinsius : petas β

---

[a] As a signal for the starting of the races in the circus.
The praetor presided.

[b] The priests and worshippers of Isis. The priests and

his white napkin,[a] Hermogenes filched the napkin
from the praetor. Nobody had brought a napkin for
fear of theft: Hermogenes filched the cloth from the
table. If this too be unavailable, Hermogenes is not
afraid to ungird the couches and the feet of the
tables. Though the seats in the theater be hot with
a burning sun, the awnings are drawn back when
Hermogenes comes in. Sailors in alarm hasten to
furl sail whenever Hermogenes appears in the har-
bor. The bald ones in their linens and the rattle-
carrying crowd[b] flee when Hermogenes takes his
stand among the worshippers. Hermogenes never
brought a napkin to dinner; from dinner Hermo-
genes always carried one back.

29 (26)

You, a senator, tread sixty thresholds of a morning;
so me, a knight, you look on as an idler because I
don't run here and there about town from daybreak
on and bring home, wearied out, a thousand kisses.
But you do it to give a new name to the purple
records[c] or to govern the peoples of Numidia or Cap-
padocia. But I, whom you would force to break off
my sleep halfway and endure and bear the morning
mud, what do I look for? When my wandering foot
leaves its broken shoe and a sudden heavy shower of
rain is falling and the slave who went off with

initiates wore linen, and their heads were shaved: Juv.
6.533.
   [c] I.e. become consul; cf. 11.4.5n.

nec venit ablatis clamatus verna lacernis,
　　accedit gelidam servus ad auriculam,
et 'rogat ut secum cenes Laetorius' inquit.
　　viginti nummis? non ego: malo famem
15　quam sit cena mihi, tibi sit provincia merces,
　　et faciamus idem nec mereamur idem.

30

Siccus, sobrius est Aper; quid ad me?
　　servum sic ego laudo, non amicum.

31

Hoc nemus, hi fontes, haec textilis umbra supini
　　palmitis, hoc riguae ductile flumen aquae,
prataque nec bifero cessura rosaria Paesto,
　　quodque viret Iani mense nec alget holus,
5　quaeque natat clusis anguilla domestica lymphis,
　　quaeque gerit similes candida turris aves,
munera sunt dominae: post septima lustra reverso
　　has Marcella domos parvaque regna dedit.
si mihi Nausicaa patrios concederet hortos,
10　Alcinoo possem dicere 'malo meos.'

31.8 has … domos $\beta\gamma$: has … dapes T : hos … lares
Heinsius

---

[a] The slave seems to have been sent ahead or on some
errand, but for what reason M. does not say.

my cloak doesn't come to my shout,[a] a flunky approaches my frozen ears and says: "Laetorius requests your company at dinner." For twenty sesterces? Not I, I prefer to go hungry rather than to be rewarded with a dinner while you get a province, so that we do the same work but don't get the same pay.

30

Aper is dry and sober. What is that to me? I commend a slave so, not a friend.[b]

31

This wood, these springs, this woven shade of overhanging vine, this ductile stream of flowing water, and the meadows and the rose beds that yield nothing to twice-flowering Paestum, and the potherbs green in January and not frostbitten, and the household eel that swims in closed water, and the white tower that harbors birds white as itself, these are the gifts of my lady. To me, when I returned after seven lusters, Marcella gave this house, this little realm. If Nausicaa were to offer me her father's gardens, I could say to Alcinous: "I prefer my own."

[b] Somewhat similarly Cicero *Att.* 7.4.1: "I am sending you Dionysius . . . an honest fellow (*frugi hominem*), and in case that sounds too much like commending a freedman, a really fine man" (but D. *was* a freedman).

32

O Iuliarum dedecus Kalendarum,
vidi, Vacerra, sarcinas tuas, vidi;
quas non retentas pensione pro bima
portabat uxor rufa crinibus septem
5   et cum sorore cana mater ingenti.
Furias putavi nocte Ditis emersas.
has tu priores frigore et fame siccus
et non recenti pallidus magis buxo
Irus tuorum temporum sequebaris.
10   migrare clivum crederes Aricinum.
ibat tripes grabatus et bipes mensa
et cum lucerna corneoque cratere
matella curto rupta latere meiebat;
foco virenti suberat amphorae cervix;
15   fuisse gerres aut inutiles maenas
odor impudicus urcei fatebatur,
qualem marinae vissit aura piscinae.
nec quadra deerat casei Tolosatis,
quadrima nigri nec corona pulei
20   calvaeque restes alioque cepisque,
nec plena turpi matris olla resina,
Summemmianae qua pilantur uxores.
quid quaeris aedes vilicosque derides,

32.17 qualem (-lis *β*) . . . uissit *βγ* : qualis . . . uix sit *cod.
Arondell.* (*saec. XV*)

I saw your movables, Vacerra, you disgrace of July's Kalends,[a] yes, I saw them. They were not impounded in lieu of two years' rent, so your wife with her seven red curls and your white-headed mother, and your burly sister were carrying them. I thought the Furies had come out from the darkness of Dis. These three went in front and you followed, parched with cold and hunger, paler than old box-wood, the Irus of your times. One would have thought that Aricia's slope[b] was moving house. Along went a three-footed truckle bed and a two-footed table, and a broken chamberpot was pissing from a chip in the side together with a lamp and a cornel-wood bowl. The neck of a flagon was lying under a green brazier. An obscenely stinking jug confessed that it had contained salt pickerel or worthless sprats, a smell such as the reek of a marine fishpond farts. Nor was there wanting a slice of Tolosan cheese, nor a four-year-old wreath of black pennyroyal, nor ropes bare of garlic and onions, nor your mother's pot full of foul turpentine, with which Summemmius'[c] wives depilate them-selves. Why do you look for a house and make mock of superintendents[d] when you could lodge for

---

[a] Quarter-day, as it were.
[b] Where beggars took their stand: cf. 2.19.3.
[c] Cf. 1.34.6n.
[d] By asking to rent a lodging without money to pay for it.

habitare gratis, o Vacerra, cum possis?
25　　haec sarcinarum pompa convenit ponti.

33

Ut pueros emeret Labienus vendidit hortos.
　　nil nisi ficetum nunc Labienus habet.

34

Triginta mihi quattuorque messes
tecum, si memini, fuere, Iuli,
quarum dulcia mixta sunt amaris,
sed iucunda tamen fuere plura;
5　　et si calculus omnis huc et illuc
diversus bicolorque digeratur,
vincet candida turba nigriorem.
si vitare voles acerba quaedam
et tristis animi cavere morsus,
10　　nulli te facias nimis sodalem:
gaudebis minus et minus dolebis.

35

Tamquam simpliciter mecum, Callistrate, vivas,
　　dicere percisum te mihi saepe soles
non es tam simplex quam vis, Callistrate, credi.
　　nam quisquis narrat talia, plura tacet.

33.1 hortos γ : agros β　　　34.8 uoles T : uelis βγ

---

[a] I.e. a bridge where beggars resort; cf. 10.5.3.
[b] Cf. 1.65.4. The "figs" on the boys are caused by

nothing, Vacerra? This procession of movables is fit for the bridge.[a]

33

To buy boys, Labienus sold a suburban estate. Now Labienus owns nothing but a fig plantation.[b]

34

I have had thirty-four summers with you, Julius,[c] if I remember. Their sweets were mingled with bitters, but still the pleasant things were the more. And if all the pebbles[d] were sorted on this side and on that into two piles of different color, the white heap would outnumber the black. If you wish to avoid certain sournesses and guard against painful heart-bites, to no man make yourself too much a friend. Less will be your joy and less your grief.

35

As though you and I were on terms of total frankness, Callistratus, it's your habit to tell me often that you have been sodomized. You are not so frank as you wish to be thought, Callistratus. For when a man tells such things, there are more things he doesn't tell.

Labienus (see SB^1). For *habet* of owning landed property see 3.48n.
[c] Martialis.
[d] Cf. 8.45.2n.

36

Libras quattuor aut duas amico
algentemque togam brevemque laenam,
interdum aureolos manu crepantis,
possint ducere qui duas Kalendas,
5   quod nemo nisi tu, Labulle, donas,
non es, crede mihi, bonus. quid ergo?
ut verum loquar, optimus malorum es.
Pisones Senecasque Memmiosque
et Crispos mihi redde, seu priores:
10 fies protinus ultimus bonorum.
vis cursu pedibusque gloriari?
Tigrim vince levemque Passerinum:
nulla est gloria praeterire asellos.

37

Nasutus nimium cupis videri.
nasutum volo, nolo polyposum.

38

Hunc qui femineis noctesque diesque cathedris

*   *   *   *   *   *   *

incedit tota notus in urbe nimis,

36.9 seu *SB*[1] : sed *β* (*deest γ*)

36

Because nobody but you, Labullus, gives a friend
four pounds or two and a chilly gown and a short
cloak and now and then some gold pieces chinking
in the hand that could last over two Kalends,[a] that
does not make you a good patron, believe me. What
then? To tell the truth, you're the best of a bad lot.
Give me back the Pisos and the Senecas and the
Memmiuses and the Crispuses, or their predeces-
sors: you will immediately become the worst of a
good lot. If you want to boast of your running and
your feet, beat Tigris and nimble Passerinus. Out-
running donkeys is nothing to brag of.

37

You are too anxious to seem a man with a nose.[b] I
like a man with a nose, I don't like a man with a
polyp.

38

This fellow here who sits beside women's chairs day
and night and is forever murmuring into some ear,
who parades perpetually in attendance on bevies of
married ladies,[c] only too well-known all over town,

---

[a] I.e. for more than a month.

[b] Cf. 1.3.6n.

[c] I translate Housman's *exempli causa* supplement
(735): *adsidet atque aliqua semper in aure sonat, / qui
matronarum iungens latus usque catervis.*

crine nitens, niger unguento, perlucidus ostro,
    ore tener, levis pectore, crure glaber,
5 uxori qui saepe tuae comes improbus haeret,
    non est quod timeas, Candide: non futuit.

39

Odi te quia bellus es, Sabelle.
res est putida bellus; et Sabellus.
bellum denique malo quam Sabellum.
tabescas utinam, Sabelle, belle!

40

Mentiris: credo. recitas mala carmina: laudo.
    cantas: canto. bibis, Pontiliane: bibo.
pedis: dissimulo. gemma vis ludere: vincor.
    res una est sine me quam facis: et taceo.
5 nil tamen omnino praestas mihi. 'mortuus' inquis
    'accipiam bene te.' nil volo: sed morere.

41

Non est, Tucca, satis quod es gulosus:
et dici cupis et cupis videri.

38.4 levis *Bowersock* : latus $\beta\gamma$: labris SB^1 39.2 *dist.* SB^1

---

[a] *Levis* and *glaber* are not synonymous. The first might refer to natural smoothness, the second implies depilation (SB^1).

[b] Untranslatable puns: *bellus* = "pretty," *Sabellus, bellum* = "war."

sleek of hair, black with pomade, transparent
in purple, tender-faced, smooth-chested, shaven-
legged[a] who often sticks unblushingly to your wife's
side—no need for alarm, Candidus. He doesn't fuck.

39

I dislike you because you are a pretty fellow,
Sabellus. A pretty fellow is a thing of disgust,
Sabellus; so is Sabellus. In fine, I prefer war to
Sabellus. May you prettily rot, Sabellus.[b]

40

You tell a lie, I believe you. You recite bad poems, I
praise them. You sing, I sing. You drink, Pontili-
anus, I drink. You fart, I pretend not to notice. You
want to play draughts, I lose. There is one thing you
do without me; I also hold my tongue.[c] But for me
you do nothing at all. "I'll treat you well when I'm
dead," you say. I don't want anything; but die.

41

It is not enough, Tucca, that you are a gourmand;
you want to be called one and you want to appear
one.[d]

[c] I.e., I won't say what that is.

[d] *Gulosus* may mean "gourmand" or "gourmet." M. uses
it of "Tucca" in the first sense; "Tucca" would like it to be
used of himself in the second.

42

Barbatus rigido nupsit Callistratus Afro
    hac qua lege viro nubere virgo solet.
praeluxere faces, velarunt flammea vultus,
    nec tua defuerunt verba, Thalasse, tibi.
5 dos etiam dicta est. nondum tibi, Roma, videtur
    hoc satis? expectas numquid ut et pariat?

43

    Facundos mihi de libidinosis
    legisti nimium, Sabelle, versus,
    quales nec Didymi sciunt puellae
    nec molles Elephantidos libelli.
5 sunt illic Veneris novae figurae,
    quales perditus audeat fututor,
    praestent et taceant quid exoleti,
    quo symplegmate quinque copulentur,
    qua plures teneantur a catena,
10 extinctam liceat quid ad lucernam.
    tanti non erat esse te disertum.

44

Unice, cognato iunctum mihi sanguine nomen,
    qui geris et studio corda propinqua meis,

---

   [a] Cf. the nuptials of Nero and Pythagoras described by
Tac. *Ann.* 15.37.

   [b] Nothing is known of them. One editor reads *Didymae*
(γ), perhaps rightly.

42

Bearded Callistratus married rugged Afer in the usual form in which a virgin marries a husband. The torches shone in front, the wedding veil covered his face, and, Thalassus, you did not lack your words. Even the dowry was declared.[a] Are you still not satisfied, Rome? Are you waiting for him to give birth?

43

You read me some all too well-turned verses about debauchees, Sabellus, such as neither Didymus' girls[b] know of nor the voluptuous little books of Elephantis. Therein are novel erotic postures such as only a desperate fornicator would venture, what male prostitutes provide and keep quiet about, in what combinations five persons are linked, by what chain are held more than five, what can go on when the lamp is put out. You paid too high a price[c] for your poetic skill.[d]

44

Unicus, you that bear a name joined to mine by kindred blood and a mind close to mine in literary pur-

[c] "Wading through all this filth" (*SB*[1]). Or perhaps *tanti* is more general: "your poetic skill does not compensate (for the vile content)."
[d] I.e. for displaying it.

carmina cum facias soli cedentia fratri,
　　pectore non minor es sed pietate prior.
5　Lesbia cum lepido te posset amare Catullo,
　　te post Nasonem blanda Corinna sequi.
nec deerant Zephyri, si te dare vela iuvaret;
　　sed tu litus amas. hoc quoque fratris habes.

45

Haedina tibi pelle contegenti
nudae tempora verticemque calvae,
festive tibi, Phoebe, dixit ille
qui dixit caput esse calceatum.

46 (47)

Difficilis facilis, iucundus acerbus es idem:
　　nec tecum possum vivere nec sine te.

47 (46)

Vendunt carmina Gallus et Lupercus.
sanos, Classice, nunc nega poetas.

44.5 lepido β : tenero γ

---

[a] Unicus (otherwise unknown) parallels Turnus in
11.10, who wrote satires to avoid competition with a

suits, you write poetry second only to your brother's;
yet your talent is no less than his, but your affection
is greater. Lesbia could have loved you along with
witty Catullus, beguiling Corinna could have fol-
lowed you after Naso. And if you had wished to
spread your sails, Zephyrs were not wanting; but
you love the shore. This too you owe your brother.[a]

45

You cover your temples and the top of your bare
bald pate with a kid's skin. It was a witty saying
when somebody told you, Phoebus, that your head is
well shod.

46 (47)

You are difficult and easy, pleasant and sour; and I
can't live with you nor yet without you.[b]

47 (46)

Gallus and Lupercus sell their poems. Now, Clas-
sicus, tell me that poets are insane.

brother who wrote tragedies. U. wrote love elegies, and
could have excelled in a more ambitious genre, but out of
brotherly affection refrained; so that this very modesty
was something he owed to his brother. M. was of course
aware of the surface meaning, "in this too you take after
your brother," but the epigram makes no sense if the
brother too was an elegist (*SB*[1]).

[b] The last line may be borrowed from Ov. *Am.* 3.11.39.

48

Boletos et aprum si tamquam vilia ponis
    et non esse putas haec mea vota, volo:
si fortunatum fieri me credis et heres
    vis scribi propter quinque Lucrina, vale.
5 lauta tamen cena est: fateor, lautissima, sed cras
    nil erit, immo hodie, protinus immo nihil,
quod sciat infelix damnatae spongea virgae
    vel quicumque canis iunctaque testa viae:
mullorum leporumque et suminis exitus hic est,
10 sulphureusque color carnificesque pedes.
non Albana mihi sit comissatio tanti
    nec Capitolinae pontificumque dapes;
imputet ipse deus nectar mihi, fiet acetum
    et Vaticani perfida vappa cadi.
15 convivas alios, cenarum, quaere, magister,
    quos capiant mensae regna superba tuae:
me meus ad subitas invitet amicus ofellas.
    haec mihi quam possum reddere cena placet.

---

[a] Used for sanitary purposes.
[b] *Qui ad vomitum accurrit*—Schrevelius.

48

If you serve mushrooms and boar as everyday fare
and don't imagine that these are the object of my
prayers, well and good; but if you think I am getting
rich and want to be made my heir because of five
Lucrine oysters, good-bye. "But it's a fine dinner":
very fine, I confess, but tomorrow it will be nothing,
or rather today, or rather a moment from now it will
be nothing; a matter for a luckless sponge on a
doomed mop stick[a] or some dog or other[b] or a crock
by the roadside[c] to take care of.[d] That is what mul-
let and hares and sow's udder come to—that and a
pasty complexion and feet that play torturer. No
Alban revel[e] would be worth it to me, no Capitoline
or Pontifical banquets.[f] Should a god himself debit
me with nectar, it would turn to vinegar and the
treacherous, flat content of a Vatican jar. Feast-
master, look for other guests to be captivated by the
proud despotism of your table. As for me, let a
friend invite me to potluck morsels. I like a dinner I
can return.

[c] Set by the roadside as a urinal. Cf. 6.93.2.

[d] Lit. "know about," here used idiomatically if the text
is sound (see SB^3).

[e] Such as Domitian gave at his Alban villa.

[f] Twice annually a "banquet of Capitoline Jupiter" was
held for the three resident deities, Jupiter, Juno, and
Minerva. The sumptuous dinners of the College of Pontiffs
were proverbial (Hor. *Od.* 2.14.28; cf. Macrob. *Sat.*
3.13.12).

49

Crinitae Line paedagoge turbae,
rerum quem dominum vocat suarum
et credit cuï Postumilla dives
gemmas, aurea, vina, concubinos:
5   sic te perpetua fide probatum
nulli non tua praeferat patrona:
succurras misero, precor, furori
et serves aliquando neglegenter
illos qui male cor meum perurunt,
10 quos et noctibus et diebus opto
in nostro cupidus sinu videre,
formosos, niveos, pares, gemellos,
grandes — non pueros, sed uniones.

50

Daphnonas, platanonas et aerios pityonas
   et non unius balnea solus habes,
et tibi centenis stat porticus alta columnis
   calcatusque tuo sub pede lucet onyx,
5 pulvereumque fugax hippodromon ungula plaudit
   et pereuntis aquae fluctus ubique sonat,
atria longa patent. sed nec cenantibus usquam
   nec somno locus est. quam bene non habitas!

49

Linus, supervisor of the long-haired troop,[a] whom
wealthy Postumilla calls master of her possessions
and to whom she entrusts jewels, gold, wine, male
concubines, so may your patroness prefer nobody to
you, tried in perpetual loyalty: I beg you, aid my
unhappy craze and for once keep negligent watch
over these beings that sorely burn my heart, that
night and day I eagerly long to see in my bosom,
these beautiful, snow-white matching twins, these
big[b]—not boys, but pearls.

50

You are sole proprietor of plantations—laurel,
plane, and airy pine—and baths not made for one;
for you stands a lofty portico with a hundred
columns, and alabaster gleams trodden under your
foot; the swift hoof strikes the dusty hippodrome
and everywhere sounds the flow of water going to
waste,[c] halls stretch at length. But there's nowhere
a place to dine or to sleep. How well you are—not
lodged!

[a] In charge of "Postumilla's" boy slaves (*paedagogus*),
he had come to manage her whole establishment.
[b] Cf. 2.48.5n.
[c] Frontin. *Aqu.* 88 *pereuntes aquae* (of fountains) is com-
pared.

51

Tam saepe nostrum decipi Fabullinum
miraris, Aule? semper homo bonus tiro est.

52

Tempora Pieria solitus redimire corona
    nec minus attonitis vox celebrata reis,
hic situs est, hic ille tuus, Sempronia, Rufus,
    cuius et ipse tui flagrat amore cinis.
5 dulcis in Elysio narraris fabula campo,
    et stupet ad raptus Tyndaris ipsa tuos:
    [tu melior quae deserto raptore redisti,
      illa virum voluit nec repetita sequi.]
ridet ut Iliacos audit Menelaus amores:
10   absolvit Phrygium vestra rapina Parim.
accipient olim cum te loca laeta piorum,
    non erit in Stygia notior umbra domo.
non aliena videt, sed amat Proserpina raptas:
    iste tibi dominam conciliabit amor.

53

Nummi cum tibi sint opesque tantae
quantas civis habet, Paterne, rarus,

52.7–8 *seclusi*   9 ut *Castiglioni* : et βγ

---

[a] Helen of Troy.

[b] The couplet appears to be interpolated; see Appendix
A.

132

51

Does it surprise you, Aulus, that our friend Fabullinus is so often taken in? A good man is always a greenhorn.

52

Here lies one who was wont to bind his brows with a Pierian garland, a voice no less famous among frightened men on trial, here, Sempronia, your Rufus, whose very dust glows with love for you. Your story, a sweet romance, is told in the Elysian Fields, and Tyndareus' daughter[a] herself is lost in amazement at your ravishing. [But you are better than she, for you forsook your ravisher and returned, whereas she would not follow her husband even when reclaimed.[b]] Menelaus smiles as he listens to a tale of Ilian love; your rape absolves Phrygian Paris. When the happy places of the virtuous shall one day receive you, there will be no more famous shade in the house of Styx. Proserpina looks with no unsympathetic eye on ravished women, she loves them.[c] Your love story will win you Her Majesty's good will.

53

Though you have money, Paternus, such wealth as few citizens possess, you give nothing away and

---

[c] For she herself was carried off by Pluto.

largiris nihil incubasque gazae
ut magnus draco, quem canunt poetae
5   custodem Scythici fuisse luci.
sed causa, ut memoras et ipse iactas,
dirae filius est rapacitatis.
ecquid tu fatuos rudesque quaeris
illudas quibus auferasque mentem?
10 huic semper vitio pater fuisti.

54

Crine ruber, niger ore, brevis pede, lumine laesus,
  rem magnam praestas, Zoile, si bonus es.

55

Gratis qui dare vos iubet, puellae,
insulsissimus improbissimusque est.
gratis ne date, basiate gratis.
hoc Aegle negat, hoc avara vendit.
5   sed vendat: bene basiare quantum est!
hoc vendit quoque nec levi rapina
— aut libram petit illa Cosmiani
aut binos quater a nova moneta —,
ne sint basia muta, ne maligna,
10 ne clusis aditum neget labellis.
humane tamen hoc facit, sed unum:
gratis quae dare basium recusat,
gratis lingere non recusat Aegle.

55.4–8 *ita dist.* SB[3]   11–12 recusat ... sed unum
Housman

brood over your treasure like the great dragon that once, as poets sing, was guardian of the Scythian grove.[a] But the reason, as you yourself relate and spread abroad, is a son of dire rapacity. Are you looking for simpletons, greenhorns whom you can fool and rob of sense? To this vice you have always been father.

54

Red-haired, black-faced, short-footed, boss-eyed, it's a great achievement, Zoilus, if you're a good fellow.

55

Anybody who tells you, girls, to give for nothing is an impudent jackass. Don't *give* for nothing, kiss for nothing. Aegle refuses this, this the greedy girl sells. But let her sell it: a good kiss is a fine thing. She even sells (and for no small taking; she asks a pound of Cosmus' scent or else eight gold pieces, fresh from the mint) that her kisses be not silent or grudging, that she not bar entrance with closed lips. But there's just one thing she's nice about; Aegle, who refuses to give a kiss for nothing, does not refuse to lick for nothing.[b]

[a] Guarding the golden fleece. "Scythian" = "Colchian."
[b] Housman (736f), whose conjecture may well be right, translates: "Yet in so doing she acts considerately; for Aegle, who refuses to give a kiss unbought (yes, even a single kiss), does not refuse . . ."

56

Aegrotas uno decies aut saepius anno,
    nec tibi sed nobis hoc, Polycharme, nocet:
nam quotiens surgis, soteria poscis amicos.
    sit pudor: aegrota iam, Polycharme, semel.

57

    Cur saepe sicci parva rura Nomenti
    laremque villae sordidum petam, quaeris?
    nec cogitandi, Sparse, nec quiescendi
    in urbe locus est pauperi. negant vitam
5   ludi magistri mane, nocte pistores,
    aerariorum marculi die toto;
    hinc otiosus sordidam quatit mensam
    Neroniana nummularius massa,
    illinc balucis malleator Hispanae
10 tritum nitenti fuste verberat saxum;
    nec turba cessat entheata Bellonae,
    nec fasciato naufragus loquax trunco,
    a matre doctus nec rogare Iudaeus,
    nec sulphuratae lippus institor mercis.
15 numerare pigri damna quis potest somni?

56

You fall sick ten times or more in a single year, and this, Polycharmus, hurts us, not you. For every time you rise from your bed, you ask your friends for getting-well presents.[a] For shame, Polycharmus, fall sick now for good and all.

57

Do you ask why I often visit my bit of land near dry Nomentum and my villa's dingy hearth? Sparsus, there's no place in Rome for a poor man to think or rest. Schoolmasters deny you life[b] in the morning, bakers at night, the hammers of the coppersmiths all day. On one hand the idle moneychanger rattles his grubby counter with Nero's metal,[c] on the other the pounder of Spanish gold dust beats his well-worn stone with shining mallet; neither does Bellona's frenzied throng give up, nor the garrulous castaway with his swaddled trunk,[d] nor the Jew that his mother taught to beg, nor the bleareyed pedlar of sulphurated wares. Who can count up the losses of lazy sleep? He will tell us how many

[a] *Soteria*, presents given to somebody on his recovery from illness.

[b] I.e. make it unbearable. *Somnum* ("sleep") might have been expected.

[c] Probably coins of low denomination issued by Nero.

[d] So pretending he had lost a limb.

dicet quot aera verberent manus urbis,
cum secta Colcho Luna vapulat rhombo.
tu, Sparse, nescis ista nec potes scire,
Petilianis delicatus in regnis,
20   cui plana summos despicit domus montis,
et rus in urbe est vinitorque Romanus
nec in Falerno colle maior autumnus,
intraque limen latus essedo cursus,
et in profundo somnus et quies nullis
25   offensa linguis, nec dies nisi admissus.
nos transeuntis nisus excitat turbae,
et ad cubile est Roma. taedio fessis
dormire quotiens libuit, imus ad villam.

58

Ancillariolum tua te vocat uxor, et ipsa
lecticariola est: estis, Alauda, pares.

59

Tantum dat tibi Roma basiorum
post annos modo quindecim reverso
quantum Lesbia non dedit Catullo.

57.26 nisus *Heinsius* : ri- $\beta\gamma$

---

[a] An eclipse was attributed to witches, and the clashing of brass vessels was in order to drive away evil demons. "Colchis" refers to Medea's sorceries.

pots and pans the hands of the City clash when the
moon is cut and beaten by the magic wheel of
Colchis.[a] You, Sparsus, know nothing of all this, nor
can you know, leading your life of luxury in your
Petilian[b] domain, where your ground floor looks
down on the hill tops and you have the country in
the town and a Roman vine-dresser and a vintage as
large as on Falernian slopes; where within your
threshold there's a broad drive for your curricle,
where there's slumber down in the depths and quiet
that no tongues disturb, and no daylight save by
admission. As for me, the thrusting of the passing
crowd awakes me and Rome is at my bedside.
Whenever I'm sick and tired of it and want to go to
sleep, I go to my villa.

58

Your wife calls you one for slave girls and she her-
self is one for litter boys.[c] You make a pair, Alauda.

59

Rome gives you a quantity of kisses, now that you
have returned after fifteen years, such as Lesbia
never gave Catullus. The whole neighborhood is

[b] So called from a previous owner.
[c] *Lecticariola*, diminutive of *lecticaria* ("fond of *lecti-
carii*"), contracted from *lecticariaria* as *bellarius* from *bel-
lariarius*.

te vicinia tota, te pilosus
5   hircoso premit osculo colonus;
hinc instat tibi textor, inde fullo,
hinc sutor modo pelle basiata,
hinc menti dominus periculosi,
†hinc† dexiocholus, inde lippus
10 fellatorque recensque cunnilingus.
iam tanti tibi non fuit redire.

60

Martis alumne dies, roseam quo lampada primum
   magnaque siderei vidimus ora dei,
si te rure coli viridisque pudebit ad aras,
   qui fueras Latia cultus in urbe mihi:
5 da veniam servire meis quod nolo Kalendis
   et qua sum genitus vivere luce volo.
natali pallere suo, ne calda Sabello
   desit, et, ut liquidum potet Alauda merum,
turbida sollicito transmittere Caecuba sacco,
10 atque inter mensas ire redire suas,

60.3 pudebit *β* : pige- *γ*   7–12 *interrog. feci*

upon you. The hairy farmer crushes you with a kiss like a billy goat's. The weaver is at you from one side, the fuller from another. Then there's the cobbler who has just kissed his leather, and the owner of a dangerous chin, and the man with the gammy right leg,[a] and he of the bleary eye, and the sucker and the licker fresh from his cunt. It really wasn't worth your while to come home.

60

Day, child of Mars, on which I first saw the rosy lamp and the mighty countenance of the starry god,[b] if you are ashamed to be celebrated in the country and at green altars whom once I worshipped in Latium's city:[c] pardon me if I do not choose to be a servant on my own Kalends and wish to *live*[d] on the day I was born. Am I to turn pale on my birthday for fear Sabellus doesn't get enough hot water[e] and to filter turbid Caecuban through an anxious bag so that Alauda drinks his wine clear? Am I to go

[a] Such persons were considered bad luck to meet. Housman (1105) cites Lucian, *Pseudol.* 17 and Pliny *N.H.* 28.35. He conjectured *hinc, Rex, dexiocholus*, but M. does not have the name Rex elsewhere and the reading remains in doubt.

[b] The Sun.

[c] M. has chosen to celebrate his birthday Kalends of March at his Nomentan villa (*rure*, v. 3) instead of in town. He is not in Spain, where he would not have had the choice.

[d] M. constantly returns to this idea: cf. 2.90.3; 5.20.11.

[e] To mix with his wine.

excipere hos illos, et tota surgere cena
marmora calcantem frigidiora gelu?
quae ratio est haec sponte sua perferre patique,
quae te si iubeat rex dominusque, neges?

61

Versus et breve vividumque carmen
in te ne faciam times, Ligurra,
et dignus cupis hoc metu videri.
sed frustra metuis cupisque frustra.
5 in tauros Libyci fremunt leones,
non sunt papilionibus molesti.
quaeras censeo, si legi laboras,
nigri fornicis ebrium poetam,
qui carbone rudi putrique creta
10 scribit carmina quae legunt cacantes.
frons haec stigmate non meo notanda est.

62

Antiqui rex magne poli mundique prioris,
sub quo pigra quies nec labor ullus erat,
nec regale nimis fulmen nec fulmine digni,
scissa nec ad Manes, sed sibi dives humus:

61.5 fremunt β : ruunt Tγ 62.4 sed sibi *Heinsius* :
sed sis γ : nec mihi β

---

[a] Diners reclined barefoot, but M. could have asked for
his slippers (cf. 3.50.3; 8.59.14). Perhaps he was in too
much of a hurry. I take vv. 7–12 as a series of questions;
cf. Cic. *Att.* 12.44.2 *quid enim? sedere totos dies in villa?*

142

to and fro among my tables receiving this guest and
that, getting to my feet all through the meal and
treading marble colder than ice?[a] Where is the
sense of enduring and suffering all this voluntarily,
things which you would refuse if your patron and
lord[b] ordered you?

61

You are afraid, Ligurra, of my writing verses
against you, a brief, lively poem, and you long to
seem worthy of such an apprehension. But idle is
your fear and idle your desire. Libyan lions roar at
bulls, they do not trouble butterflies. I advise you, if
you are anxious to be read of, to look for some boozy
poet of the dark archway who writes verses with
rough charcoal or crumbling chalk which folk read
while they shit. This brow of yours is not for mark-
ing with *my* brand.

62

Great king of ancient heaven and a bygone world,
under whom was idle repose, no toil, no too regal
thunderbolts, nor any that deserved them, nor was
the ground cloven down to the underworld but kept
its riches for itself:[c] come, happy and kind, to these

[b] Cf. 1.112.1.
[c] There was no mining for precious metals.

5   laetus ad haec facilisque veni sollemnia Prisci
      gaudia: cum sacris te decet esse tuis.
   tu reducem patriae sexta, pater optime, bruma
      pacifici Latia reddis ab urbe Numae.
   cernis ut Ausonio similis tibi pompa macello
10   pendeat et quantus luxurietur honos?
   quam non parca manus largaeque nomismata mensae,
      quae, Saturne, tibi pernumerentur opes?
   utque sit his pretium meritis et gratia maior,
      et pater et frugi sic tua sacra colit.
15   at tu, sancte — tuo sic semper amere Decembri —
      hos illi iubeas saepe redire dies.

63

Uncto Corduba laetior Venafro,
Histra nec minus absoluta testa,
albi quae superas oves Galaesi
nullo murice nec cruore mendax,
5   sed tinctis gregibus colore vivo:

customary joys of Priscus.[a] It is fitting that you be
with your rites. You bring him back to his father-
land in the sixth midwinter, best of fathers, from
pacific Numa's Latin city. Do you see how an array[b]
like an Ausonian market hangs aloft in your honor,
how magnificent the luxurious revel, how unstint-
ing the hand and the tokens[c] of the lavish board,
what riches, Saturn, are counted out to you? And to
add value and esteem to these benefactions, it is a
father[d] and a man of thrift who thus celebrates your
rites. But do you, holy one (so may you ever be loved
in your own December), bid these days often return
for him.

63

Corduba, more fruitful than oily Venafrum and no
less perfect than Istria's jars, surpassing the sheep
of white Galaesus, not false with shellfish or blood
but whose flocks are tinted with living color:[e] tell

[a] Priscus (see Appendix A) used to give a feast annually
at the Saturnalia.

[b] The "wealthy cord" of 8.78.7.

[c] Representing presents to be taken away by guests
(*apophorêta*). The fourteenth book is wholly concerned
with such.

[d] As a *paterfamilias*, Priscus would not ordinarily
indulge in such extravagance. *Pater* also seems to pick up
pater optime in v. 7.

[e] Cf. 5.37.7n.

dic vestro, rogo, sit pudor poetae
nec gratis recitet meos libellos.
ferrem, si faceret bonus poeta,
cui possem dare mutuos dolores.
10   corrumpit sine talione caelebs,
caecus perdere non potest quod aufert:
nil est deterius latrone nudo:
nil securius est malo poeta.

64

Vincentem roseos facieque comaque ministros
    Cinna cocum fecit. Cinna gulosus homo est.

65

Formosa Phyllis nocte cum mihi tota
se praestitisset omnibus modis largam,
et cogitarem mane quod darem munus,
utrumne Cosmi, Nicerotis an libram,
5   an Baeticarum pondus acre lanarum,
an de moneta Caesaris decem flavos:
amplexa collum basioque tam longo
blandita quam sunt nuptiae columbarum,
rogare coepit Phyllis amphoram vini.

64.2 est Tβ : es γ

your poet, I pray you, to have some compunction and not to recite my little books gratis.[a] I could bear this if a good poet did it, to whom I could return tit for tat. But a bachelor seduces without reprisal, a blind man cannot lose what he takes.[b] There's nothing worse than a naked robber, nothing more secure than a bad poet.

64

A boy more beautiful in face and hair than his rose-cheeked pages Cinna has made a cook. Cinna is a greedy fellow.[c]

65

Fair Phyllis had given herself to me all night long, generously in every way. In the morning, as I was considering what present I should give her (should it be a pound of Cosmus or Niceros or a swingeing weight of Baetic wool or ten yellow boys from Caesar's mint?), Phyllis put her arms round my neck and, coaxing me with a kiss as lingering as the nuptials of doves, started to ask for a jar of wine.

[a] Whether as a plagiarist, pretending they were his own, or simply to amuse the audience (the equivalent of a breach of copyright).

[b] I.e. an eye; but M. ought to have said so. *quod aufert* could represent a gloss, *quem aufert*, which has ousted *ocellum* from the text (*SB*[3]).

[c] Thinking of nothing but food; cf. 12.41.1n.

66

Bis quinquagenis domus est tibi milibus empta,
    vendere quam summa vel breviore cupis.
arte sed emptorem vafra corrumpis, Amoene,
    et casa divitiis ambitiosa latet.
5 gemmantes prima fulgent testudine lecti
    et Maurusiaci pondera rara citri;
argentum atque aurum non simplex Delphica portat
    stant pueri dominos quos precer esse meos.
deinde ducenta sonas et ais non esse minoris.
10   instructam vili vendis, Amoene, domum.

67

Maiae Mercurium creastis Idus,
Augustis redit Idibus Diana,
Octobres Maro consecravit Idus.
Idus saepe colas et has et illas,
5 qui magni celebras Maronis Idus.

68

Matutine cliens, urbis mihi causa relictae,
    atria, si sapias, ambitiosa colas.

---

[a] Cf. 5.57n.

[b] M. ironically assumes (knowing better of course) that the price includes the furnishings.

[c] May 15 was the dedication day of the temple of Mercury; Aug. 13 that of the temple of Diana on the Aventine; and Oct. 15 the birthday of Virgil.

66

You bought a house for twice fifty thousand which
you want to sell even for a lesser sum. But you
seduce the buyer with a crafty trick, Amoenus; a cot-
tage is concealed by ostentatious wealth. Jewelled
couches gleam with first-class tortoiseshell, and
Moorish citrus wood, massive and choice. A three-
legged table of complex design bears silver and gold.
Boys stand about whom I would fain have as my
"Masters."[a] Then you boom about two hundred
thousand and say it's worth no less. You are selling
a furnished house cheap, Amoenus.[b]

67

The Ides of May created Mercury. Diana returns on
the Ides of August. Maro made sacred the Ides of
October.[c] May you often keep these Ides and those,
you who celebrate great Maro's Ides.[d]

68

Morning client, reason why I left Rome,[e] if you were
sensible, you would dance attendance on preten-

[d] The epigram need not be addressed to any particular
person, though Silius was doubtless in mind; cf. 11.50.

[e] M. had left Rome because he was weary of the duties
of a client. Now a client is pestering him to plead in court.

non sum ego causidicus nec amaris litibus aptus,
sed piger et senior Pieridumque comes;
5 otia me somnusque iuvant, quae magna negavit
Roma mihi: redeo, si vigilatur et hic.

69

Sic tamquam tabulas scyphosque, Paule,
omnes archetypos habes amicos.

70

Lintea ferret Apro vatius cum vernula nuper
et supra togulam lusca sederet anus
atque olei stillam daret enterocelicus unctor,
udorum tetricus censor et asper erat:
5 frangendos calices effundendumque Falernum
clamabat biberet quod modo lotus eques.
a sene sed postquam patruo venere trecenta,
sobrius a thermis nescit abire domum.
o quantum diatreta valent et quinque comati!
10 tunc, cum pauper erat, non sitiebat Aper.

71

Nil non, Lygde, mihi negas roganti:
at quondam mihi, Lygde, nil negabas.

---

a *Habes* means (a) "have" and (b) "think." It is covertly
implied that "Paulus" is no better a judge of people than of
antiques (*SB*[3]).

tious halls. I am no advocate nor apt for bitter lawsuits, but lazy and elderly and a companion of the Pierian maids. I am fond of leisure and sleep, which great Rome denied me. If I'm kept awake here too, I go back.

69

Paulus, to you your friends are all genuine, like your pictures and cups.[a]

70

Not long ago, when a bow-legged, home-bred slave carried Aper's towels and a one-eyed old woman sat watching over his little gown and a ruptured masseur handed him his drop of oil, he was a stern, harsh censor of boozers. He would shout that the cups should be smashed and the Falernian poured away which a knight, fresh from his bath, was imbibing. But now that three hundred thousand has come his way from an aged uncle, he doesn't know how to go home from the baths sober. Oh, what a difference open-work goblets and five long-haired boys can make! When Aper was poor, he wasn't thirsty.

71

There is nothing you do not refuse me when I ask, Lygdus; but once, Lygdus, you refused me nothing.[b]

[b] Cf. 4.12n.

72

Iugera mercatus prope busta latentis agelli
　　et male compactae culmina fulta casae,
deseris urbanas, tua praedia, Pannyche, lites
　　parvaque, sed tritae praemia certa togae.
5　frumentum, milium tisanamque fabamque solebas
　　vendere pragmaticus, nunc emis agricola.

73

Heredem tibi me, Catulle, dicis.
non credo nisi legero, Catulle.

74

Dum tibi Niliacus portat crystalla cataplus,
　　accipe de circo pocula Flaminio.
hi magis audaces, an sunt qui talia mittunt
　　munera? sed gemmis vilibus usus inest:
5　nullum sollicitant haec, Flacce, toreumata furem,
　　et nimium calidis non vitiantur aquis.

73.2 credo β : -dam γ　　　74.4 gemmis *vel* geminis βγ :
-nus *Gruter*

---

[a] On one of the great roads leading out of Rome. The
little farm lay hidden behind them.

[b] *Credam* used to be the accepted reading, but the
present is idiomatic; cf. K.–S. I.119f.

[c] I.e. in the will, which would be after Catullus' death.
A hint to him to die.

[d] See Index under Flaminius.

[e] *Audaces calices* were cups not valuable enough to

72

Having bought the acres of a little farm that crouches near the tombs[a] and the propped-up roof of a jerry-built cottage, you forsake the city lawsuits that were your landed properties, Pannychus, and the small but sure rewards of your threadbare gown. As an attorney you used to sell wheat and millet and barley and beans; now as a farmer you buy them.

73

You say I am your heir, Catullus. I won't believe it[b] unless I read it,[c] Catullus.

74

While a shipment from the Nile is bringing you crystal, accept some cups from the Flaminian Circus.[d] Are they the bolder,[e] or those who send such presents? And yet, cheap goblets[f] have their usefulness. These chasings[g] don't interest a thief, Flaccus, and are not damaged by too hot water. Besides, the

cause anxiety as to breakage: cf. 14.94. It is a "bold" thing to send such cups to a man that imports crystal.

[f] *Gemma* often means a jewelled vessel, sometimes one made of precious material such as murrine or even of glass (4.22.6); cf. 8.68.5. Here ironically of earthenware (cf. 14.94), unless *geminus* (Gruter) is read, as in older editions ("cheap goblets have two advantages").

[g] Lit. "chased cups." But *toreumata* may be ironic, the cups in fact being plain, or used loosely; cf. 4.46.16n.

quid quod securo potat conviva ministro
    et casum tremulae non timuere manus?
hoc quoque non nihil est, quod propinabis in istis,
10   frangendus fuerit si tibi, Flacce, calix.

75

    Festinat Polytimus ad puellas;
    invitus puerum fatetur Hymnus;
    pastas glande natis habet Secundus;
    mollis Dindymus est, sed esse non vult;
5   Amphion potuit puella nasci.
    horum delicias superbiamque
    et fastus querulos, Avite, malo
    quam dotis mihi quinquies ducena.

76

Amphora vigesis, modius datur aere quaterno.
ebrius et crudus nil habet agricola.

77

    Multis dum precibus Iovem salutat
    stans summos resupinus usque in ungues
    Aethon in Capitolio, pepedit.
    riserunt homines, sed ipse divum
5   offensus genitor trinoctiali
    affecit domicenio clientem.

75.2 hymnus β : hypnus γ 7 Avite *Heinsius* : aui γ :
amice β

---

    [a] As having been defiled by impure lips: cf. 2.15 and
Anth. Pal. 11.39.   [b] He is impatient to become a man.

guest drinks and the page isn't nervous, and shaky
hands don't fear a fall. This too counts for some-
thing: you will pledge in these, Flaccus, if you are
going to have to break the cup.[a]

75

Polytimus is hurrying to the girls,[b] Hymnus doesn't
like admitting that he's a boy, Secundus has but-
tocks acorn-sated,[c] Didymus is effeminate but
doesn't want to be, Amphion could have been born a
girl.[d] Avitus, I would rather have their whims and
haughtiness and querulous disdains than five times
two hundred thousand sesterces of dowry.

76

A jar of wine goes for twenty asses, a peck of wheat
for four. Drunk and dyspeptic, the farmer has
nothing.[e]

77

As Aethon on the Capitol addressed Jupiter with
many a prayer, standing on tiptoe and bending
backwards, he farted. People laughed, but the
father of the gods himself was offended and pun-
ished our client with three nights of home dining.[f]

[c] There is a play in the Latin on *glans*, acorn or the like,
and *glans penis*. "Secundus'" *nates* have had their fill.

[d] So loath is he to oblige *more puerili*.

[e] He has more food and wine than he can use, but they
have no market value.

[f] Aethon was a parasite.

post hoc flagitium misellus Aethon,
cum vult in Capitolium venire,
sellas ante petit Paterclianas
10 et pedit deciesque viciesque.
sed quamvis sibi caverit crepando,
compressis natibus Iovem salutat.

78

Nil in te scripsi, Bithynice. credere non vis
et iurare iubes? malo satisfacere.

79

Donavi tibi multa quae rogasti;
donavi tibi plura quam rogasti:
non cessas tamen usque me rogare.
quisquis nil negat, Atticilla, fellat.

80

Ne laudet dignos, laudat Callistratus omnes.
cui malus est nemo, quis bonus esse potest?

After this scandal, when poor little Aethon wants to go to the Capitol, he first visits Paterclus' latrines and farts ten times or twenty. But though he has covered himself by thus breaking wind, he addresses Jupiter buttocks clenched.

78

I have written nothing against you, Bithynicus. You choose not to believe me and tell me to swear? I prefer to pay.[a]

79

I have given you much that you asked for. I have given you more than you asked for. Yet you go on and on asking me. Whoever refuses nothing, Atticilla, is a sucker.[b]

80

To avoid praising those who deserve it, Callistratus praises everybody. Who can be good in the eyes of a man to whom nobody is bad?

[a] A plaintiff was entitled by Roman law to challenge the defendant to take an oath as to the justice of his own case, refusal being treated as tantamount to an admission of the plaintiff's claim. Thus a debtor must deny the debt or pay it. M. ironically pretends to regard himself as owing "Bithynicus" the offensive epigram which the latter accuses him of having written (and would really like him to write? Cf. 5.60).

[b] Cf. 4.12n.

81

Brumae diebus feriisque Saturni
mittebat Umber aliculam mihi pauper;
nunc mittit alicam: factus est enim dives.

82

Effugere in thermis et circa balnea non est
    Menogenen, omni tu licet arte velis.
captabit tepidum dextra laevaque trigonem,
    imputet exceptas ut tibi saepe pilas.
5 colliget et referet laxum de pulvere follem,
    etsi iam lotus, iam soleatus erit.
lintea si sumes, nive candidiora loquetur,
    sint licet infantis sordidiora sinu.
exiguos secto comentem dente capillos
10   dicet Achilleas disposuisse comas.
fumosae feret ipse propin de faece lagonae
    frontis et umorem colliget usque tuae.
omnia laudabit, mirabitur omnia, donec
    perpessus dicas taedia mille 'veni!'

82.4 exceptas γ : acc- β

---

[a] The point of the epigram is that *alicula*, the first gift, is *in form* a diminutive of *alica* (spelt water: cf. 13.6), whereas in fact *alica* is a smaller gift than *alicula*.

[b] On *thermae* and *balnea* see Sp. 2.7n.

[c] On this and the follis (v. 5) see 4.19n.

81

In the days of midwinter and Saturn's holiday
Umber used to send me a light coat. He was a poor
man. Now he sends me spelt water, for he has
become rich.[a]

82

To escape Menogenes in the public baths and
around the private baths[b] is not possible, try what
device you will. He will grab at the warm trigon[c]
with right and left so that he can often score a point
to you for the balls he catches.[d] He'll collect from the
dust and bring back the loose follis, even if he has
already bathed and already put on his slippers. If
you take your towels, he'll say they are whiter than
snow, though they be dirtier than a baby's lap. As
you comb your scanty hair with the split ivory, he'll
say you have arranged locks of Achilles. He'll fetch
you an aperitif[e] with his own hands from the dregs
of a smoky flagon and continually wipe the moisture
from your forehead. He'll praise everything, admire
everything, until after enduring a thousand annoy-
ances you say: "Come to dinner."

[d] Menogenes catches balls which the player has let go
by and scores them to him.

[e] *Propin*, from Greek προπ(ι)εῖν (propiein; "drink before-
hand").

83

Derisor Fabianus hirnearum,
omnes quem modo colei timebant
dicentem tumidas in hydrocelas
quantum nec duo dicerent Catulli,
5   in thermis subito Neronianis
vidit se miser et tacere coepit.

84

Nolueram, Polytime, tuos violare capillos,
  sed iuvat hoc precibus me tribuisse tuis.
talis eras modo tonse Pelops positisque nitebas
  crinibus, ut totum sponsa videret ebur.

85

Pediconibus os olere dicis.
hoc si, sicut ais, Fabulle, verum est,
quid tu credis olere cunnilingis?

86

Triginta tibi sunt pueri totidemque puellae:
una est nec surgit mentula. quid facies?

87

Bis Cotta soleas perdidisse se questus,
dum neglegentem ducit ad pedes vernam,

83

Fabianus, mocker of hernias, of whom till lately all testicles went in fear as he inveighed against tumid ruptures more fluently than two Catulluses,[a] all of a sudden, poor fellow, saw himself in Nero's baths—and fell silent.

84

I was loth, Polytimus, to spoil your hair, but I am glad I yielded to your prayers. Such was Pelops newly shorn, thus he shone when his hair was laid aside, so that his bride-to-be saw all the ivory.

85

You say that sodomites smell at the mouth. If what you say is true, Fabullus, where do you think cunt-lickers smell?

86

You have thirty boys and as many girls; you have one cock, and it doesn't rise. What will you do?

87

Cotta complained that he had twice lost his slippers, as he brought with him a careless slave-attendant,

[a] A writer of mimes; cf. 5.30.3.

qui solus inopi praestat et facit turbam,
excogitavit — homo sagax et astutus —
5   ne facere posset tale saepius damnum:
excalceatus ire coepit ad cenam.

88

Tongilianus habet nasum: scio, non nego. sed iam
nil praeter nasum Tongilianus habet.

89

Quod lana caput alligas, Charine,
non aures tibi sed dolent capilli.

90

Pro sene, sed clare, votum Maro fecit amico,
cui gravis et fervens hemitritaeos erat,
si Stygias aeger non esset missus ad umbras,
ut caderet magno victima grata Iovi.
5   coeperunt certam medici spondere salutem.
ne votum solvat nunc Maro vota facit.

whose single self provides and makes up his staff, he being a poor man. Sagacious, cunning fellow that he is, he thought out a way to avoid a repetition of such a loss. He started going to dinner barefoot.[a]

88

Tongilianus has a nose, I know it, I don't deny it. But by now Tongilianus has nothing but a nose.[b]

89

You wrap your head in wool, Charinus. It's not your ears that hurt, but your hair.[c]

90

Maro made a vow, made it loud and clear,[d] for an aged friend suffering from a severe, burning semitertian, that, if the sick man was not sent to the shades of Styx, a welcome victim would fall to great Jupiter. The doctors have begun to guarantee a certain recovery. Maro now makes vows against having to pay his vow.

[a] The point consists simply in the ludicrous naiveté of his expedient—going to dinner barefoot—after the reader has been led to expect a masterpiece of cunning (SB^1). Naturally he would not need to put on slippers if he had nothing on his feet to begin with (diners reclined barefoot).

[b] Cf. 1.3.6n.

[c] Charinus swathes his head to conceal his baldness.

[d] As a *captator* he wished the sick man to hear of it.

91

Communis tibi cum viro, Magulla,
cum sit lectulus et sit exoletus,
quare, dic mihi, non sit et minister.
suspiras; ratio est, times lagonam.

92

Saepe rogare soles qualis sim, Prisce, futurus,
    si fiam locuples simque repente potens.
quemquam posse putas mores narrare futuros?
    dic mihi, si fias tu leo, qualis eris?

93

Qua moechum ratione basiaret
coram coniuge repperit Labulla.
parvum basiat usque morionem;
hunc multis rapit osculis madentem
5 moechus protinus et suis repletum
ridenti dominae statim remittit.
quanto morio maior est maritus!

94

Scribebamus epos; coepisti scribere: cessi,
    aemula ne starent carmina nostra tuis.

91

Since you share a couch and a male concubine with your husband, Magulla, tell me why you don't share a page too. You sigh. There's a reason, you're afraid of the flagon.[a]

92

You are wont to ask me, Priscus, what sort of person I should be if I were suddenly to become rich and powerful. Do you suppose that anybody can foretell his character? Tell me, if you were to become a lion, what would *you* be like?

93

Labulla has found a way to kiss her lover in her husband's presence. She keeps on kissing her dwarf fool. The lover immediately catches hold of him while he is still damp with many kisses and sends him back charged with his own kisses to the smiling lady of the house. How much greater a fool is the husband!

94

I was writing an epic; you started to write one. I gave up, so that my poetry should not stand in com-

---

[a] I.e. poison.

transtulit ad tragicos se nostra Thalia cothurnos:
    aptasti longum tu quoque syrma tibi.
5 fila lyrae movi Calabris exculta Camenis:
    plectra rapis nobis, ambitiose, nova.
audemus saturas: Lucilius esse laboras.
    ludo levis elegos: tu quoque ludis idem.
quid minus esse potest? epigrammata fingere coepi:
10   hinc etiam petitur iam mea palma tibi.
elige quid nolis — quis enim pudor omnia velle? —
    et si quid non vis, Tucca, relinque mihi.

95

    Musseti pathicissimos libellos,
    qui certant Sybariticis libellis,
    et tinctas sale pruriente chartas
    Istanti lege Rufe; sed puella
5   sit tecum tua, ne thalassionem
    indicas manibus libidinosis
    et fias sine femina maritus.

96

Cum tibi nota tui sit vita fidesque mariti
    nec premat ulla tuos sollicitetve toros,
quid quasi paelicibus torqueris inepta ministris,
    in quibus et brevis est et fugitiva Venus?

95.4 Istanti *Munro* : inst- Tβγ (*cf. ad* 7.68)

---

[a] Here simply = "Muse."
[b] Cf. 5.30.2n.

petition with yours. My Thalia[a] transferred herself
to tragic buskins; you too fitted the long train on
yourself. I stirred the lyre strings, as practised by
Calabrian Muses;[b] eager to show off, you snatch my
new quill away from me. I try my hand at satire;
you labor to be Lucilius. I play with light elegy; you
play with it too. What can be humbler? I start
shaping epigrams; here too you are already after my
trophy. Choose what you don't want (modesty for-
bids us to want everything), and if there's anything
you don't want, Tucca, leave it for me.

95

Read, Istantius Rufus, the ultra-pathic little books
of Mussetius, which vie with the little books of
Sybaris,[c] pages tinged with prurient wit. But have
your girl with you, lest you make lustful hands sing
your wedding song and become a husband without a
woman.

96

Since your husband's life and fidelity is known to
you and no other woman presses or threatens your
marriage bed, why do you foolishly torture yourself
because of pages, as though they were your rivals?

[c] Doubtless the *Sybaritica* mentioned by Ovid in *Trist.*
2.417. The author was one Hemitheon, called "The Sybar-
ite" (Lucian, *Adv. indoctum* 23; *Pseudolog.* 3). Mussetius is
unknown.

5   plus tibi quam domino pueros praestare probabo:
     hi faciunt ut sis femina sola viro;
    hi dant quod non vis uxor dare. 'do tamen,' inquis,
     'ne vagus a thalamis coniugis erret amor.'
    non eadem res est: Chiam volo, nolo mariscam:
10   ne dubites quae sit Chia, marisca tua est.
    scire suos fines matrona et femina debet:
     cede sua pueris, utere parte tua.

97

    Uxor cum tibi sit puella qualem
    votis vix petat improbis maritus,
    dives, nobilis, erudita, casta,
    rumpis, Basse, latus, sed in comatis,
5   uxoris tibi dote quos parasti.
    et sic ad dominam reversa languet
    multis mentula milibus redempta
    ut nec vocibus excitata blandis
    molli pollice nec rogata surgat.
10   sit tandem pudor aut eamus in ius.
    non est haec tua, Basse: vendidisti.

97.2 inprobis ς : -bus βγ   8 ut nec SB^3 : uel ne (*pro* ut
nec? *Lindsay*) : sed nec β   9 surgat SB^3 : -git βγ

Such affairs are short and fleeting. I shall show you that the boys do more for you than for their master. Thanks to them you are the only woman for your husband. They give him what you his wife don't want to give. "But I *will* give it," you say, "so that my spouse's love doesn't go gadding from our bedroom." That is not the same thing. I want a Chian fig, not one of the big sort. And in case you are in any doubt as to which is the Chian, the big one is yours. A married lady and a woman ought to know her limitations. Leave their part[a] to the boys and use yours.

97

Your wife is a girl such as a husband would hardly ask for in his most extravagant prayers, rich, noble, cultivated, virtuous. You burst your loins, Bassus, but you do it with long-haired boys whom you have procured for yourself with your wife's dowry. And your cock, which she bought for many thousands, returns to your lady so languid that, whether excited by coaxing words or requested with a soft thumb, it won't rise. Have some shame, for a change; or let us go to law. It's not yours, Bassus. You sold it.

[a] With a double sense, "role" and "part (of body)"; cf. *SB*[1].

98

Baetis olivifera crinem redimite corona,
  aurea qui nitidis vellera tinguis aquis;
quem Bromius, quem Pallas amat; cui rector aquaru̇
  Albula navigerum per freta pandit iter:
5 ominibus laetis vestras Istantius oras
  intret et hic populis ut prior annus eat.
non ignorat onus quod sit succedere Macro;
  qui sua metitur pondera, ferre potest.

98.5 Istantius *Munro* : instantibus γ : intran- *vel* instran- β
(*cf. ad* 7.68)

98

Baetis, your hair wreathed with crown of olive,
coloring golden fleeces with your shining waters,
loved by Bromius, loved by Pallas; for whom
Albula,[a] ruler of waters, opens a ship-bearing path
through the seas: may Istantius enter the shores of
Spain[b] with happy omens and may this year pass for
its peoples like the last. He knows what a burden it
is to succeed Macer. Who measures his load, can
bear it.

[a] Old name of the Tiber, called by Virgil (*Aen.* 8.77)
"lord (*regnator*) of western waters." He receives at Ostia
the merchandise of Baetica after its journey overseas
(*SB*[3]).

[b] *Vestras = Baeticorum.*

[LIBER XIII]

XENIA

1

Ne toga cordylis et paenula desit olivis
    aut inopem metuat sordida blatta famem,
perdite Niliacas, Musae, mea damna, papyros:
    postulat ecce novos ebria bruma sales.
5   non mea magnanimo depugnat tessera talo,
    senio nec nostrum cum cane quassat ebur:
haec mihi charta nuces, haec est mihi charta fritillus:
    alea nec damnum nec facit ista lucrum.

2

Nasutus sis usque licet, sis denique nasus,
    quantum noluerit ferre rogatus Atlans,

1.5 talo *βγ* : telo T   2.2 noluerit *vett.* : -rat T*βγ*

[a] Alan Ker seems to have been right in holding that this epigram and the next do not belong in this book.
[b] I.e. use up papyrus, which in due course will become wrappers for fish or olives, or be devoured by insects.

BOOK XIII

MOTTOS

1[a]

That tunny-fry may not lack a gown and olives an
overcoat, nor the uncleanly bookworm fear penuri-
ous hunger, waste some papyrus from the Nile, ye
Muses[b]—the loss is mine. See, tipsy midwinter calls
for new jests. My dice do not contend with high-
hearted knucklebones,[c] nor do sice and ace[d] shake
my ivory. This paper is my nuts, this paper my dice
box; such gambling brings neither loss nor gain.

2

Your nose[e] may be large as you please, you may *be* a
nose, a nose so big that Atlas[f] would not want to

[c] Obscure, but the general sense is clear: M. does not
gamble with dice or knucklebones, nor yet with nuts (cf.
4.66.15f).

[d] The number six and the number one (called *canis*, the
dog).

[e] Cf. 1.3.6n.

[f] Who bore the weight of heaven.

et possis ipsum tu deridere Latinum:
    non potes in nugas dicere plura meas
5 ipse ego quam dixi. quid dentem dente iuvabit
    rodere? carne opus est, si satur esse velis.
ne perdas operam: qui se mirantur, in illos
    virus habe, nos haec novimus esse nihil.
non tamen hoc nimium nihil est, si candidus aure
10   nec matutina si mihi fronte venis.

3

Omnis in hoc gracili Xeniorum turba libello
    constabit nummis quattuor empta tibi.
quattuor est nimium? poterit constare duobus,
    et faciet lucrum bybliopola Tryphon.
5 hac licet hospitibus pro munere disticha mittas,
    si tibi tam rarus quam mihi nummus erit.
addita per titulos sua nomina rebus habebis:
    praetereas, si quid non facit ad stomachum.

4 Tus

Serus ut aetheriae Germanicus imperet aulae
    utque diu terris, da pia tura Iovi.

carry it if he were asked, you may be able to make mock of Latinus himself, but you can't say more against my trifles than I have said myself. Why gnaw tooth with tooth?[a] You need flesh if you want to fill your stomach. Don't waste your efforts: keep your venom for self-admirers. *I* know that these things of mine are nothing—and yet not altogether nothing if you come to me with a friendly ear and a countenance not matutinal.[b]

3

The entire assembly of Mottos in this slender little book will cost you four sesterces to buy. Is four too much? It could cost two, and bookseller Trypho still make a profit. You can send these couplets to your guests instead of a gift, if sesterces are as scarce with you as they are with me. You will find each item[c] identified by its title; if anything is not to your taste, just pass it by.

4. Incense

That Germanicus rule the palace of the skies late in time and long rule the earth, give pious incense to Jupiter.

[a] Attacking me is like grinding your teeth—no satisfaction in it.

[b] I.e. sober and serious; cf. 4.8.12; 11.17.

[c] The gifts to which the mottos were to be attached.

5 Piper

Cerea quae patulo lucet ficedula lumbo
  cum tibi sorte datur, si sapis, adde piper.

6 Alica

Nos alicam, poterit mulsum tibi mittere dives.
  si tibi noluerit mittere dives, emes.

7 Faba

Si spumet rubra conchis tibi pallida testa,
  lautorum cenis saepe negare potes.

8 Far

Imbue plebeias Clusinis pultibus ollas,
  ut satur in vacuis dulcia musta bibas.

9 Lens

Accipe Niliacem, Pelusia munera, lentem:
  vilior est alica, carior illa faba.

10 Simila

Nec dotes similae possis numerare nec usus,
  pistori totiens cum sit et apta coco.

6.2 emes α : -emis β : eme γ 　　7.2 nempe *Heinsius*

5. Pepper

When a shiny wax-colored beccafico with ample loins is given you by lot, if you are wise, add pepper.

6. Spelt water

I can send you spelt water,[a] a rich man will be able to send you mead. If the rich man won't send it, then buy!

7. Beans

If pale beans froth for you in a red pot, you can often say no to the dinners of the high-livers.

8. Groats

Impregnate common jars with porridge from Clusium, so that after dinner you may drink sweet new wine from them empty.[b]

9. Lentils

Receive Nile lentils, a present from Pelusium;[c] they're cheaper than spelt, dearer than beans.

10. Flour

Impossible to count the properties and uses of flour, since it so often comes in handy for the baker and the cook.

[a] Cf. 12.81.3.
[b] *Puls* was seemingly supposed to ripen new wine.
[c] Celebrated for its lentils: Virg. *Georg.* 1.228.

MARTIAL

11 Hordeum

Mulio quod non det tacituris, accipe, mulis.
    haec ego coponi, non tibi, dona dedi.

12 Frumentum

Tercentum Libyci modios de messe coloni
    sume, suburbanus ne moriatur ager.

13 Betae

Ut sapiant fatuae, fabrorum prandia, betae,
    o quam saepe petet vina piperque cocus!

14 Lactucae

Cludere quae cenas lactuca solebat avorum,
    dic mihi, cur nostras inchoat illa dapes?

15 Ligna acapna

Si vicina tibi Nomento rura coluntur,
    ad villam moneo, rustice, ligna feras.

16 Rapa

Haec tibi brumali gaudentia frigore rapa
    quae damus, in caelo Romulus esse solet.

11.2 dedi Tγ : dabo β

---

[a] The muleteer steals the barley and sells it to the inn-keeper.

[b] I.e. go barren by being over-cropped, and not allowed to lie fallow. The gift of Libyan corn will maintain the

178

11. Barley

Receive something for your muleteer *not* to give his mules—they won't talk. This gift I have given not you but the innkeeper.[a]

12. Corn

Take three hundred pecks from the harvest of the Libyan farmer, lest your land near the city die.[b]

13. Beet

To give some flavor to insipid beet, the workman's lunch, how often will the cook ask for wine and pepper!

14. Lettuces

The lettuce that used to wind up our forebears' dinners, tell me, why does it begin *our* meals?[c]

15. Smokeless wood

If you farm fields near Nomentum, I advise you, countryman, to bring the wood to your farmhouse.[d]

16. Rapes

These rapes that I give you, delighting in midwinter cold, Romulus is wont to eat in heaven.[e]

farmer for a time. But the quantity seems suspiciously large.

[c] Cf. 11.52.5.   [d] See Appendix A.

[e] The deified Romulus retains his simple tastes in heaven; cf. Sen. *Apoc.* 9.

17 Fascis coliculi

Ne tibi pallentes moveant fastidia caules,
    nitrata viridis brassica fiat aqua.

18 Porri sectivi

Fila Tarentini graviter redolentia porri
    edisti quotiens, oscula clusa dato.

19 Porri capitati

Mittit praecipuos nemoralis Aricia porros:
    in niveo virides stipite cerne comas.

20 Napi

Hos Amiternus ager felicibus educat hortis:
    Nursinas poteris parcius esse pilas.

21 Asparagi

Mollis in aequorea quae crevit spina Ravenna
    non erit incultis gratior asparagis.

---

[a] I.e. *porrum sectivum*; cf. 10.48.9.
[b] But according to Pliny (*N.H.* 19.110) the finest came
from Egypt, those from Ostia and Aricia ranking next (K).
[c] The navew is also called the French turnip (*Napus*

17. Bundle of cabbage sprouts

Lest the pale sprouts disgust you, let the cabbage turn green with water and soda.

18. Cut leeks

When you have eaten the strong-smelling shoots[a] of Tarentine leek, give your kisses closed.

19. Headed leeks

Bosky Aricia sends outstanding leeks.[b] Observe the green leaves on the snow-white stem.

20. Navews

These the land of Amiternum matures in its fertile gardens. You will be able to eat the balls of Nursia more sparingly.[c]

21. Asparagus

The soft stalk that grew in seaside Ravenna[d] will not be more palatable than wild asparagus.

brassica), in Greek ῥάφυς or βουνιάς, and has a root elongated like a carrot. It likes a sloping situation, and a light and dry soil, whereas the ordinary rape thrives in the marsh: Colum. 2.10. Amiternum was famed for them, and Nursia came second (Pliny *N.H.* 19.77) (K).

[d] Which often produced asparagus of three to the pound: Pliny *N.H.* 19.54. According to Athenaeus (62e) the planted asparagus grew to a great size, but the best were not the cultivated. The wild was called *corruda* (Pliny) (K).

22 Uvae duracinae

Non habilis cyathis et inutilis uva Lyaeo,
    sed non potanti me tibi nectar ero.

23 Ficus Chiae

Chia seni similis Baccho, quem Setia misit,
    ipsa merum secum portat et ipsa salem.

24 Cydonea

Si tibi Cecropio saturata Cydonea melle
    ponentur, dicas 'haec melimela' licet.

25 Nuces pineae

Poma sumus Cybeles: procul hinc discede, viator,
    ne cadat in miserum nostra ruina caput.

26 Sorba

Sorba sumus, molles nimium tendentia ventres:
    aptius haec puero quam tibi poma dabis.

24.2 licet $\beta\gamma$: placent a

---

[a] These grapes were kept to be eaten, and not turned into wine. The temperate Augustus speaks of himself (Suet. *Aug.* 76.2) as eating in his litter an ounce of bread and a few *duracinae* (K).

BOOK XIII

22. Hard grapes

I am a grape unfit for the wine cup and useless to Lyaeus; but if you don't drink me, I shall be nectar to you.[a]

23. Chian figs

The Chian fig is like old wine sent by Setia; it carries wine with itself and salt with itself.[b]

24. Quinces

If quinces steeped in Cecropian honey are set in front of you, you can say: "These are honey apples."

25. Pine cones

We are Cybele's fruits;[c] go hence, traveller, last our fall come down upon your luckless head.

26. Sorb apples

We are sorb apples, tautening too loose bellies. You will do better to give this fruit to your boy[d] than to yourself.

[b] The Chian fig was not only pungent (cf. 7.25.8), but also juicy (K).
[c] Because she turned her favorite Attis into a fir, which thus became sacred to her.
[d] I.e. *cinaedo*.

27 Petalium caryotarum

Aurea porrigitur Iani caryota Kalendis;
    sed tamen hoc munus pauperis esse solet.

28 Vas cottanorum

Haec tibi quae torta venerunt condita meta,
    si maiora forent cottana, ficus erat.

29 Vas Damascenorum

Pruna peregrinae carie rugosa senectae
    sume: solent duri solvere ventris onus.

30 Caseus Lunensis

Caseus Etruscae signatus imagine Lunae
    praestabit pueris prandia mille tuis.

31 Caseus Vestinus

Si sine carne voles ientacula sumere frugi,
    haec tibi Vestino de grege massa venit.

27 lemm. petalium γ : -adium β : -auiuum T

---

[a] But see *petalium* in *OLD*.
[b] By poor clients to their patrons: cf. 8.33.11f.

27. Stem (?)[a] of dates

A golden date is offered on the Kalends of January;[b] and yet this is usually the gift of a poor man.

28. Jar of Syrian figs

These Syrians, that have come to you stored in a twisted cone, would be figs if they were larger.[c]

29. Jar of damsons

Take plums wrinkled by shrivelling old age in foreign parts;[d] they are wont to dissolve the load of a constipated stomach.

30. Luna cheese

A cheese marked with the image of Etruscan Luna[e] will afford your boys a thousand lunches.[f]

31. Vestine cheese

If you wish to take a frugal, meatless breakfast, this hunk comes to you from a Vestine flock.

[c] *Cottana* were small figs from Syria: Pliny *N.H.* 13.51. Cf. 4.88.6 and 7.53.7.

[d] Plums of Damascus; cf. 5.18.3. Pliny (*N.H.* 15.43) says that those grown in Italy did not shrink "because their native suns are lacking."

[e] No doubt a crescent.

[f] Cheeses were made very large at Luna. Pliny *N.H.* 11.241 says they were made of a thousand pounds' weight.

32 Caseus fumosus

Non quemcumque focum nec fumum caseus omnem,
    sed Velabrensem qui bibit, ille sapit.

33 Casei Trebulani

Trebula nos genuit; commendat gratia duplex,
    sive levi flamma sive domamur aqua.

34 Bulbi

Cum sit anus coniunx et sint tibi mortua membra,
    nil aliud bulbis quam satur esse potes.

35 Lucanicae

Filia Picenae venio Lucanica porcae:
    pultibus hinc niveis grata corona datur.

36 Cistella olivarum

Haec quae Picenis venit subducta trapetis
    inchoat atque eadem finit oliva dapes.

---

[a] Athenaeus refers (113c) to this cheese by its Latin name, τῷ φουμώσῳ φυρῷ.

[b] One of several towns so called, probably on the borders of Samnium and Campania; cf. 5.71.1.

32. Smoked cheese[a]

The cheese that has imbibed not just any hearth, not every smoke, but Velabran, that cheese has savor.

33. Trebula cheeses

Trebula[b] gave us birth. A double attraction commends us, whether we are lightly toasted or soaked in water.

34. Onions

Since your wife is an old woman and your member lifeless, all you can do is to stuff yourself with onions.[c]

35. Lucanian sausages

I come, a Lucanian sausage,[d] daughter of a Picene sow; hence is given a welcome garnish to white porridge.

36. Small box of olives

These olives, that came taken from Picene presses, begin meals and also finish them.

[c] Eaten as aphrodisiacs; cf. 3.75.3; Athen. 63e.
[d] Cf. 4.46.8; 5.78.9. According to Apicius (2.4) the sausage was compounded of minced pork flavoured with pepper, cumin, savory, rue, parsley, and bay leaves. It was called in Low Latin *salsicia*, whence the word sausage (K).

37 Mala citrea

Aut Corcyraei sunt haec de frondibus horti,
  aut haec Massyli poma draconis erant.

38 Colustrum

Surripuit pastor quae nondum stantibus haedis
  de primo matrum lacte colustra damus.

39 Haedus

Lascivum pecus et viridi non utile Baccho
  det poenas; nocuit iam tener ille deo.

40 Ova

Candida si croceos circumfluit unda vitellos,
  Hesperius scombri temperet ova liquor.

41 Porcellus lactans

Lacte mero pastum pigrae mihi matris alumnum
  ponat, et Aetolo de sue dives edat.

---

[a] They were either from Alcinous' garden (cf. 10.94.2) or
were golden fruits of the Hesperides.

[b] The first milk given by the mother. It was considered
harmful to lambs (Colum. 7.3.17), and presumably to kids.

BOOK XIII

37. Citrons

These fruits are either from the branches of Corcyra's garden or they were the Massylian dragon's.[a]

38. Beestings

I give beestings,[b] abstracted by the shepherd from kids not yet able to stand, coming from the first milk of their dams.

39. Kid

Let the wanton animal, mischievous to the green vine, pay his penalty; young though he be, he has already harmed the god.[c]

40. Eggs

If white fluid surrounds yellow yokes, let the Hesperian[d] liquid of the mackerel[e] season the eggs.

41. Sucking pig

Let a rich man set before me the nursling of a lazy mother, fed on pure milk, and eat of the Aetolian boar.[f]

[c] Cf. 3.24.1f; 8.50.12.
[d] I.e. Spanish.
[e] I.e. *garum*: cf. 13.102.
[f] Like that slain by Meleager: cf. 7.27.2. If my host gives me sucking pig, he is welcome to the boar.

42 Apyrina et tubures

Non tibi de Libycis tubures et apyrina ramis,
    de Nomentanis sed damus arboribus.

43 Idem

Lecta suburbanis mittuntur apyrina ramis
    et vernae tubures. quid tibi cum Libycis?

44 Sumen

Esse putes nondum sumen; sic ubere largo
    effluit et vivo lacte papilla tumet.

45 Pulli gallinacei

Si Libycae nobis volucres et Phasides essent,
    acciperes; at nunc accipe chortis aves.

46 Persica praecocia

Vilia maternis fueramus Persica ramis:
    nunc in adoptivis Persica cara sumus.

44.2 effluit et ς : et fluit et T : -uet et β : -uet γ

---

[a] According to Pliny (*N.H.* 15.47) a kind of African fruit
of two kinds, one white, the other red. Both were probably
the jujube, *Zizyphus vulgaris*. At Verona grew a variety
called *lanata* from having a down like a peach (K).

[b] Pliny says (*N.H.* 15.47) the jujube was introduced into
Italy by Sextus Papinius, *quem consulem vidimus.*

42. Soft-seeded pomegranates and jujubes

I give jujubes[a] and soft-seeded pomegranates, not from Libyan branches but from trees of Nomentum.

43. The same

Picked from suburban branches are sent soft-seeded pomegranates and home-grown jujubes.[b] What do you want with Libyan?

44. Sow's udder

You would think it not yet udder;[c] in such abundance flows the pap, swelling with living milk.

45. Chickens

If I had Libyan birds[d] and pheasants, you should receive them. But as it is, receive fowl of the farmyard.

46 Early peaches[e]

On our mother's branches we had been peaches of little worth; now, on adoptive boughs, we are peaches of price.

[c] I.e. not yet the cooked dish but part of the living animal.

[d] Guinea fowl.

[e] According to Friedländer, peaches grafted on an apricot tree; cf. Calp. 2.42, of peaches grafted on a plum tree. Rather perhaps on a superior kind of peach (Steier, *RE* XIX.1.1025).

MARTIAL

47 Panes Picentini

Picentina Ceres niveo sic nectare crescit
    ut levis accepta spongea turget aqua.

48 Boleti

Argentum atque aurum facile est laenamque togamque
    mittere; boletos mittere difficile est.

49 Ficedulae

Cum me ficus alat, cum pascar dulcibus uvis,
    cur potius nomen non dedit uva mihi?

50 Terrae tubera

Rumpimus altricem tenero quae vertice terram
    tubera, boletis poma secunda sumus.

51 Turdorum decuria

Texta rosis fortasse tibi vel divite nardo,
    at mihi de turdis facta corona placet.

---

[a] According to Pliny, Picenian bread was made of spelt
(*alica*), steeped for nine days, then mixed with raisin juice,
and kneaded into the shape of a spool of wool (*in speciem
tractae*), and then baked. He adds that it was not fit to eat
till it had been moistened with milk mixed with honey
(*mulsum*). Pliny *N.H.* 18.50, 71, 106, 109, 112, and else-
where (K).

47. Picene loaves

Picene bread grows bigger with its white nectar, as a light sponge swells when it has taken water.[a]

48. Mushrooms

It is easy to send silver and gold and a cloak and a gown, but sending mushrooms is difficult.[b]

49. Beccaficos

Though the fig nourish me, yet, since I feed on sweet grapes, why did not the grape rather give me my name?[c]

50. Truffles

We truffles, who break the earth that nourishes us with our tender heads,[d] are produce second only to mushrooms.

51. Decade of thrushes

Perhaps you may like a garland woven of roses or rich nard, but I like one made of thrushes.[e]

[b] One is so reluctant to part with them.

[c] "Why am I not called *uvedula?*" Cf. 14.121.

[d] They grow of their own accord, particularly in dry and sandy soil (K).

[e] Fieldfares were often strung around a hoop: cf. 3.47.10 (K).

52 Anates

Tota quidem ponatur anas, sed pectore tantum
 et cervice sapit: cetera redde coco.

53 Turtures

Cum pinguis mihi turtur erit, lactuca valebis;
 et cocleas tibi habe. perdere nolo famem.

54 Perna

Cerretana mihi fiat vel missa licebit
 de Menapis: lauti de petasone vorent.

55 Petaso

Musteus est: propera, caros nec differ amicos.
 nam mihi cum vetulo sit petasone nihil.

56 Volva

Te fortasse magis capiat de virgine porca,
 me materna gravi de sue vulva capit.

57 Colocasia

Niliacum ridebis holus lanasque sequaces,
 improba cum morsu fila manuque trahes.

---

^a By eating the lettuce and snails at the *gustatio* (K).
^b I.e. defy?
^c Cf. 8.33.13. *Colocasia antiquorum.* Pliny (*N.H.* 21.87)
says it is "*caule araneoso in mandendo,*" i.e. like spider's
webs. (There is some confusion here with Indian lotus,
Nelumbo nucifera; cf. 21.174.) (K).

BOOK XIII

52. Ducks

Let a duck be served whole, but it is tasty only in the breast and neck. Return the rest to the cook.

53. Turtledoves

When I have a plump turtledove, good-bye, lettuce. And you may keep the snails. I don't want to waste my appetite.[a]

54. Gammon

Let me have Cerretanian gammon or gammon sent from the Menapians. Let gourmets wolf on ham.

55. Ham

It is fresh-cured. Be quick, don't put your dear friends off; for I want nothing to do with an aged ham.

56. Womb

Perhaps a womb from a virgin pig may be more your fancy, but a maternal one from a pregnant sow is mine.

57. Egyptian bean

You will laugh at[b] the Nile vegetable with its pliant threads when with tooth and hand you draw the unconscionable filaments.[c]

58 Iecur anserinum

Aspice quam tumeat magno iecur ansere maius!
    miratus dices: 'hoc, rogo, crevit ubi?'

59 Glires

Tota mihi dormitur hiems et pinguior illo
    tempore sum quo me nil nisi somnus alit.

60 Cuniculi

Gaudet in effossis habitare cuniculus antris.
    monstravit tacitas hostibus ille vias.

61 Attagenae

Inter sapores fertur alitum primus
Ionicarum gustus attagenarum.

62 Gallinae altiles

Pascitur et dulci facilis gallina farina,
    pascitur et tenebris. ingeniosa gula est.

---

[a] Geese were fattened on figs: cf. Hor. *Sat.* 2.8.88. The practice is recalled by the word *fegato*, Italian for liver (K).

[b] Cf. 3.58.36. Dormice were kept in pens (*gliraria*), and, for purposes of fattening, even in casks: Varro *R.R.* 3.15. They were fattened on beechnuts: Pliny *N.H.* 16.18 (K).

58. Goose liver

See how the liver swells larger than the big goose.
You will say in astonishment: "Where, pray, did this
grow?"[a]

59. Dormice

I sleep all through the winter and am fatter in the
season when only sleep gives me nourishment.[b]

60. Rabbits

The rabbit rejoices to live in dug-out caverns. He
showed hidden routes to enemies.[c]

61. Heathcocks

Among flavors of fowl the taste of Ionian heathcocks
is said to rank first.[d]

62. Fatted hens

The accommodating hen is fed on sweetened meal
and on darkness.[e] Ingenious is the palate!

[c] As though siege tunnels (actually called *cuniculi*) were
devised in imitation of rabbit burrows.

[d] So, according to Pliny, *N.H.* 10.133, who says the
attagen was formerly a rare bird, but in his day was found
in Gaul and Spain and in the Alps (K).

[e] Seneca, *Epist.* 122.4, says that fowl are kept in the
dark so that they stay still and fatten easily.

MARTIAL

63 Capones

Ne nimis exhausto macresceret inguine gallus,
    amisit testes. nunc mihi gallus erit.

64 Idem

Succumbit sterili frustra gallina marito.
    hunc matris Cybeles esse decebat avem.

65 Perdices

Ponitur Ausoniis avis haec rarissima mensis:
    hanc in piscina ludere saepe soles.

66 Columbini

Ne violes teneras periuro dente columbas,
    tradita si Cnidiae sunt tibi sacra deae.

67 Palumbi

Inguina torquati tardant hebetantque palumbi:
    non edat hanc volucrem qui cupit esse salax.

65.2 in piscina ludere R : in lautorum condere β : in l-
madere γ 66. lemm. columbini $\beta\gamma$: -n(a)e R l periuro
Rβ : perduro γ : *fort.* praed-   2 si Cnidiae *scripsi* : sic
nitidae β : si gnidiae Rγ

---

[a] Untranslatable play on two meanings of *gallus*: (a) a
cockerel. (b) a Gaul or Galatian, hence a priest of Cybele,
hence a eunuch.

63. Capons

Lest the cockerel grow thin by over-draining his loins, he has lost his testicles. Now I shall consider him a—cockerel.[a]

64. The same

In vain the hen succumbs to her sterile husband. He should have been Mother Cybele's bird.[b]

65. Partridges

This bird is very rarely served on Ausonian tables. This you are wont often to play in the pool.[c]

66. Doves

Harm not with perjured[d] tooth the tender doves, if the rites of the goddess of Cnidus have been entrusted to you.[e]

67. Ringdoves

Ringdoves retard and dull the loins. Let him who would be salacious not eat this bird.

[b] See previous note.

[c] Probably alluding to an indelicate water game (cf. πέρδομαι perdomai = "fart").

[d] Sense doubtful. Perhaps *praeduro* ("very hard") should be read.

[e] I.e. if you have been initiated into Venus' mysteries. Doves were sacred to her.

68 Galbuli

Galbina decipitur calamis et retibus ales,
    turget adhuc viridi cum rudis uva mero.

69 Cattae

Pannonicas nobis numquam dedit Umbria cattas:
    mavult haec domino mittere dona Pudens.

70 Pavones

Miraris, quotiens gemmantis explicat alas,
    et potes hunc saevo tradere, dure, coco?

71 Phoenicopteri

Dat mihi pinna rubens nomen, sed lingua gulosis
    nostra sapit. quid si garrula lingua foret?

72 Phasinae

Argoa primum sum transportata carina.
    ante mihi notum nil nisi Phasis erat.

68.1 galbina Tβ : -bula γ 69.2 domino Rγ : -n(a)e β

---

[a] The identity of the bird, here called yellow, is very
obscure. It is generally supposed to be the same as the
ἴκτερος, and has been variously identified with the golden
oriole, the greenfinch, the stone-curlew, and the green
woodpecker (K).

68. Yellow birds

The yellow bird[a] is deceived by rods[b] and nets when the young grape is swelling with wine still green.

69. Catta birds

Umbria never gave us Pannonian catta birds. Pudens prefers to send these gifts to his "master."[c]

70. Peacocks

Do you admire him whenever he spreads his jewelled wings, and can you hand him over, callous man, to the cruel cook?

71. Flamingoes

My ruddy wing[d] gives me a name, but my tongue is a treat to epicures. What if my tongue were to tell tales?[e]

72. Pheasants

I was first transported by Argo's keel. Before that I knew nothing but Phasis.

[b] Limed canes: cf. 9.54.3; 14.218 (K).

[c] The catta must be a species of bird native to Pannonia. Pudens, who came from Umbria, sent a brace or more to a favorite boy slave (cf. 1.31; 5.48; 8.63). For "master" see 5.57.2n.

[d] Phoenicopterus = "scarlet-wing."

[e] It could tell how impure was the mouth of the consumer (so Housman, 738).

73 Numidicae

Ansere Romano quamvis satur Hannibal esset,
  ipse suas numquam barbarus edit aves.

74 Anseres

Haec servavit avis Tarpei templa Tonantis.
  miraris? nondum fecerat illa deus.

75 Grues

Turbabis versus nec littera tota volabit,
  unam perdideris si Palamedis avem.

76 Rusticulae

Rustica sim an perdix quid refert, si sapor idem est?
  carior est perdix. sic sapit illa magis.

77 Cycni

Dulcia defecta modulatur carmina lingua
  cantator cycnus funeris ipse sui.

---

[a] I.e. while in Italy, where they had not yet been introduced.

[b] Cf. 9.31. Domitian had rebuilt the Temple of Jupiter Capitolinus, which was therefore safe for all time.

73. Guinea fowl

Though Hannibal had his fill of Roman goose, the barbarian never ate his own birds.[a]

74. Geese

This bird saved the Tarpeian temple of the Thunderer. Do you wonder? Not yet had a god built it.[b]

75. Cranes

You will confuse the lines and the writing[c] will not fly complete, if you lose one of Palamedes' birds.

76. Woodcock

Whether I am woodcock or partridge, what does it matter if the flavor is the same? Partridge costs more; that's how it tastes better.[d]

77. Swans

The swan, chanter of its own death, modulates sweet songs with failing tongue.

[c] *Littera* is better taken as "writing," as in 14.5, than as "letter (of the alphabet)." *Versus* can mean (a) lines or rows, (b) lines of writing, (c) verses. On Palamedes see 9.12.7n. M. was evidently thinking of Luc. 5.716 *et turbata perit dispersis littera pennis.*

[d] Cf. *magis illa iuvant quae pluris emuntur*, Juv. 11.16. Also Hor. *Sat.* 2.2.25.

78 Porphyriones

Nomen habet magni volucris tam parva Gigantis?
et nomen prasini Porphyrionis habet.

79 Mulli vivi

Spirat in advecto sed iam piger aequore mullus
languescit. vivum da mare, fortis erit.

80 Murenae

Quae natat in Siculo grandis murena profundo,
non valet exustam mergere sole cutem.

81 Rhombi

Quamvis lata gerat patella rhombum,
rhombus latior est tamen patella.

82 Ostrea

Ebria Baiano veni modo concha Lucrino:
nobile nunc sitio luxuriosa garum.

---

[a] The porphyrion is unknown. It was a bird with a long
and narrow neck, and long legs. The beak and legs were
red. So Pliny, *N.H.* 10.129 and 11.201. It is distinguished
from the pelican in Arist. *Av.* 881. According to Athen.
(388b–d) it came from Libya, and was also a domestic bird
(K).

[b] One of the giants who made war on the gods.

[c] A charioteer.

[d] Mullet were brought to table alive in glass jars so that

78. Porphyrions

Has so small a bird[a] the name of a great giant?[b] It also has the name of Porphyrion of the Green.[c]

79. Live mullets

The mullet breathes in the seawater brought along with him,[d] but already he is torpid and languishing. Give him the living sea, and he will be strong.

80. Murries

The big murry that swims in the Sicilian deep has not strength to submerge its sun-scorched skin.[e]

81. Turbot

However wide the dish that bears the turbot, yet the turbot is wider than the dish.

82. Oysters

A shellfish, I have just arrived, drunk with Baian Lucrine.[f] Now in my extravagance I thirst for noble garum.[g]

the guests could watch their color changing as they died from lack of oxygen (Sen. *N.Q.* 3.17.2).

[e] According to Aristotle (*H.A.* 8.3.4), turtles, when their shells were scorched by the sun, were unable to sink, and so were caught. M. says the same thing of the murry (K).

[f] Which produced the finest oysters: cf. 3.60.3; Macrob. *Sat.* 3.15.3.

[g] Cf. 6.93.6n.

83 Squillae

Caeruleus nos Liris amat, quem silva Maricae
    protegit: hinc squillae maxima turba sumus.

84 Scarus

Hic scarus, aequoreis qui venit adesus ab undis,
    visceribus bonus est, cetera vile sapit.

85 Coracinus

Princeps Niliaci raperis, coracine, macelli:
    Pellaeae prior est gloria nulla gulae.

86 Echini

Iste licet digitos testudine pungat acuta,
    cortice deposita mollis echinus erit.

87 Murices

Sanguine de nostro tinctas, ingrate, lacernas
    induis, et non est hoc satis: esca sumus.

87.1 de] bis *Heinsius*

---

[a] *Sparisoma cretense.* It was a favorite fish, brought originally, according to Pliny (*N.H.* 9.62) by Tiberius from the Carpathian Sea, and planted by Optatus, *praefectus classis*, in the sea between Ostia and Campania. Athenaeus (319e–320c) gives a description (K).

[b] This is Tilapia Nilotica; cf. Pliny 5.51; 9.68; 32.56. He says it was not caught in winter except on the same few days. See also Athen. 302b–309a. It was regarded as in every way superior to the *mullus*: Athenaeus 121c (K).

[c] Pellaean = Macedonian = Alexandrian.

83. Prawns

Blue Liris, whom Marica's wood protects, loves us.
From hence are we prawns, a mighty throng.

84. Parrot wrasse

This parrot wrasse[a] that came eroded by sea waves
is good as to the entrails, but for the rest it has a
poor flavor.

85. Bolti

Leader in Nile's market, bolti,[b] you are snatched up.
No glory of Pella's[c] palate outranks you.

86. Sea urchins

Though the sea urchin[d] pricks the fingers with its
sharp shell, once the carapace is put aside, it will be
soft.

87. Murexes

Ingrate, you don cloaks dyed in our blood[e] and that
is not enough: we are something to eat.[f]

[d] It was eaten with vinegar and honey sauce, parsley,
and mint (Athen. 91 a).

[e] Heinsius' conjecture *bis* ("twice") for *de*, adopted in my
edition, is attractive but not necessary.

[f] Pliny says that luxury had made the fish as precious
as pearls. Travellers speak of a hill still standing at
Tarentum of the debris of the *murex*. Cf. Col. 8.16.7; Hor.
Sat. 2.4.32 (K).

88 Gobii

In Venetis sint lauta licet convivia terris,
principium cenae gobius esse solet.

89 Lupus

Laneus Euganei lupus excipit ora Timavi,
aequoreo dulces cum sale pastus aquas.

90 Aurata

Non omnis laudes pretiumque aurata meretur,
sed cui solus erit concha Lucrina cibus.

91 Acipensis

Ad Palatinas acipensem mittite mensas:
ambrosias ornent munera rara dapes.

---

[a] Small fish, ordinarily little esteemed, but common in
the lagoons of Venice. Inferior to a blenny: Diog. L. 2.67.
Juv. (11.37) treats the price of a *gobius* as an insignificant
sum, as compared with the price of a *mullus*. The name
gobio includes also the freshwater gudgeon (K).

[b] The most prized *lupi* were called *lanati* or *lanei* from
the whiteness and softness of their flesh: Pliny *N.H.* 9.57,
61, 169. The *lupus* is the sea bass, one name of which is
the sea wolf, from its rapaciousness (K).

[c] The same as the Greek Χρύσοφρυς ("gold-eyebrow"), the
zoological name of which is now *Sparus aurata*. See Pliny
N.H. 32.43, 145, 152 (K).

BOOK XIII

88. Gobies

In Venetian parts, though the dinner may be elegant, the goby[a] is generally the start of the meal.

89. Sea bass

The woolly bass[b] breasts the mouths of Euganean Timavus, fed on fresh water with sea salt.

90. Gilthead

Not every gilthead[c] deserves praise and price, only the one whose sole food shall be Lucrine shellfish.

91. Sturgeon

Send sturgeon[d] to Palatine tables; gifts so rare should adorn ambrosial feasts.[e]

[d] According to Pliny (*N.H.* 9.60) the fish, though rare, was little esteemed in his time.

[e] I.e. of the Emperor. M. anticipates the English common law whereby "whales and sturgeons are royal fish, and belong to the King by his prerogative": 7 *Coke's Reports*, 16 A. Macrob. (*Sat.* 3.16.7–8) says that at a banquet of the Emperor Septimius Severus, the fish was ushered in by crowned attendants to the sound of flutes, *quasi numinis pompa* (K).

92 Lepores

Inter aves turdus, si quid me iudice certum est,
inter quadripedes mattea prima lepus.

93 Aper

Qui Diomedeis metuendus saetiger agris
Aetola cecidit cuspide, talis erat.

94 Dammae

Dente timetur aper, defendunt cornua cervum:
imbelles dammae quid nisi praeda sumus?

95 Oryx

Matutinarum non ultima praeda ferarum,
saevus oryx constat quot mihi morte canum!

96 Cervus

Hic erat ille tuo domitus, Cyparisse, capistro.
An magis iste tuus, Silvia, cervus erat?

---

[a] Meleager's, who slew the Calydonian boar: cf. 9.48.6;
11.69.10.

[b] Cf. 8.67.4.

[c] A one-horned, cloven-hoofed animal, not unlike a wild
goat: Pliny *N.H.* 11.255. It was a ferocious animal, and
came from Gaetulia: Opp. *De Ven.* 2.445. Its flesh was
esteemed by rich epicures: Juv. 11.140. The scimitar-
horned antelope (K).

[d] C., having by accident shot his favorite stag, prayed
the gods to grant him perpetual grief, and was turned into

BOOK XIII

92. Hares

Among birds the thrush, if anything I decide is certain, is the prime delicacy; among quadrupeds, the hare.

93. Boar

The bristly one, terror of Diomede's land, that fell by an Aetolian spear[a]—such was he.

94. Does

The boar is feared for his tusks, his horns defend the stag: unwarlike does, what are we but quarry?

95. Oryx

Not the meanest quarry among the beasts in the morning shows,[b] the savage oryx[c] cost me the death of how many hounds!

96. Stag

Was this the stag your halter tamed, Cyparissus?[d] Or rather, was he yours, Silvia?[e]

a cypress, the symbol of mourning: Ov. *Met.* 10.109 *et seqq.* (K).

[e] Daughter of Tyrrheus, huntsman of King Latinus. Ascanius, son of Aeneas, shot her pet stag, thus causing the war between the Trojans and the Latins: Virg. *Aen.* 7.483ff.

97 Lalisio

Dum tener est onager solaque lalisio matre
   pascitur, hoc infans sed breve nomen habet.

98 (99) Caprea

Pendentem summa capream de rupe videbis,
   casuram speres. decipit illa canes.

99 (98) Dorcas

Delicium parvo donabis dorcada nato:
   iactatis solet hanc mittere turba togis.

100 Onager

Pulcher adest onager. mitti venatio debet
   dentis Erythraei: iam removete sinus.

101 Oleum Venafrum

Hoc tibi Campani sudavit baca Venafri:
   unguentum quotiens sumis, et istud oles.

98.2 decipit γ : despicit $\alpha\beta$ 101.2 oles *Cod. saec. XII* :
olet T$\beta\gamma$

---

[a] Pliny (*N.H.* 8.174) says that the flesh of the *lalisio* was
much appreciated.

[b] When weaned it is called a wild ass (K).

[c] On the reading see *SB*[3].

[d] In the amphitheater. The crowd waved their togas (or
handkerchiefs; cf. 12.28.8) as a signal to let the animal go;
see following note.

97. Foal of wild ass

While he is a young wild ass and fed only by his
mother, the infant *lalisio*[a] has this name, but not for
long.[b]

98. Roe deer

Should you see the roe deer poised on the summit of
a crag, you would think she was about to fall. She's
fooling the hounds.[c]

99. Gazelle

You will give the gazelle as a pet to your small son.
The crowd is wont to let her go, waving their
gowns.[d]

100. Wild ass

Here comes the handsome wild ass. The hunt of the
Erythraean tusk should be dismissed. Now pluck
back[e] your gowns.

101. Oil of Venafrum

This the berry of Campanian Venafrum[f] has dis-
tilled for you. Whenever you use unguent, you smell
of this too.

[e] Not "shake," but "pluck back (in order to shake)"; see
SB[1]. The spectators would wave their togas as a signal to
stop the elephant hunt (not to supplicate for its return).
[f] Celebrated for its olives: cf. 12.63; Hor. *Od.* 2.6.16.

102 Garum sociorum

Expirantis adhuc scombri de sanguine primo
accipe fastosum, munera cara, garum.

103 Amphora muriae

Antipolitani, fateor, sum filia thynni:
essem si scombri, non tibi missa forem.

104 Mel Atticum

Hoc tibi Thesei populatrix misit Hymetti
Pallados a silvis nobile nectar apis.

105 Favi Siculi

Cum dederis Siculos mediae de collibus Hyblae,
Cecropios dicas tu licet esse favos.

106 Passum

Gnosia Minoae genuit vindemia Cretae
hoc tibi, quod mulsum pauperis esse solet.

---

[a] *Garum*, made of the intestines and offal of mackerel. The finest was called *garum sociorum*, and came from a manufactory at New Carthage in Spain: Pliny *N.H.* 31.93f (K).

[b] I.e. I am the inferior fish sauce called *muria*, made of the entrails of other fish than mackerel, principally tunny (K).

[c] But to somebody more important.

102. Garum of the allies[a]

Receive lordly garum, an expensive present, from the first blood of a mackerel still breathing its last.

103. Jar of muria

I am the daughter, I admit it, of Antipolitan tunny.[b] Had I been of mackerel, I should not have been sent to you.[c]

104. Attic honey

This noble nectar has been sent to you by the bee, ravager of Thesean Hymettus, from the woods of Pallas.

105. Sicilian honeycombs

When you give Sicilian combs from the heart of Hybla's hills,[d] you may say they are Cecropian.[e]

106. Raisin wine

A Gnosian vintage of Minoan Crete produced this for you. It is wont to be the poor man's mead.[f]

[d] Sicilian honey was inferior to Attic, though Hyblan and Hymettian honey are constantly mentioned together: cf. 11.42.3 (K).

[e] They are good enough to pass as such; cf. 13.117 and 1.105.4.

[f] *Mulsum* was wine and honey mixed: cf. Ep. 108. *Passum* was made from a grape called *apiana* (? muscatel) dried in the sun (K).

107 Picatum

Haec de vitifera venisse picata Vienna
ne dubites, misit Romulus ipse mihi.

108 Mulsum

Attica nectareum turbatis mella Falernum.
misceri decet hoc a Ganymede merum.

109 Albanum

Hoc de Caesareis mitis vindemia cellis
misit, Iuleo quae sibi monte placet.

110 Surrentinum

Surentina bibis? nec murrina picta nec aurum
sume: dabunt calices haec tibi vina suos.

111 Falernum

De Sinuessanis venerunt Massica prelis:
condita quo quaeris consule? nullus erat.

ᵃ Vienne in *Gallia Narbonensis*. The district bore vines
producing wine with a natural taste of pitch (K).

ᵇ A vintner in this area, whose name occurs in an
inscription (*CIL* XII.5686.752).

ᶜ To blend with honey the wine had to be old: Pliny *N.H.*
22.113 (K).

ᵈ It was inferior only to Falernian and Setine: Pliny
N.H. 14.59. One variety was sweet (Athen. 26d). Juv.
(13.214) speaks of its *pretiosa senectus* (K).

107. Retsina

Lest you doubt that this resinous wine came from Vienna,[a] Romulus[b] himself sent it to me.

108. Mead

Attic honey thickens nectarous[c] Falernian. This wine might fittingly be mixed by Ganymede.

109. Alban

A mild vintage sent this from Caesar's cellars, one that prides itself on the Julian mountain.[d]

110. Surrentine

Do you drink Surrentine?[e] Take no painted murrine or gold. These wines will give you their native cups.[f]

111. Falernian

Massic has come from the presses of Sinuessa.[g] Laid down under what consul, you ask? There wasn't one.[h]

[e] Tiberius called it generous vinegar, and Claudius noble vapidity: Pliny *N.H.* 14.64. It was a thin wine, suitable for invalids (K).

[f] Surrentine earthenware: cf. 14.102; 8.6.2.

[g] In Campania, near Mons Massicus and Mons Falernus.

[h] The wine was as old as the Roman kings!

112 Setinum

Pendula Pomptinos quae spectat Setia campos,
  exigua vetulos misit ab urbe cados.

113 Fundanum

Haec Fundana tulit felix autumnus Opimi.
  expressit mustum consul et ipse bibit.

114 Trifolinum

Non sum de primo, fateor, Trifolina Lyaeo
  inter vina tamen septima vitis ero.

115 Caecubum

Caecuba Fundanis generosa cocuntur Amyclis,
  vitis et in media nata palude viret.

116 Signinum

Potabis liquidum Signina morantia ventrem?
  ne nimium sistas, sit tibi parca sitis.

116.2 sistas sit *marg. Bongarsii* : sitias sit β : sis tanti γ :
sistant sit ς

---

[a] As though Opimius, consul in 121 B.C., had been one of
the ancient worthies who did their own farm work (cf.
6.64.2).

[b] From the district of Trifolium near Naples, a favorite
with the Emperor Augustus (Pliny *N.H.* 14.61). It had an
earthy taste (Athen. 26e). Pliny (*N.H.* 14.69) makes it a
plebeian wine, though better than most others in the area,
nor is Juvenal's reference (9.56) specially complimentary.

112. Setine

Setia, that perched aloft looks down upon the Pontine flats, sent old jars from a tiny city.

113. Fundan

Opimius' rich autumn bore this wine of Fundi. The consul pressed out the must and drank it himself.[a]

114. Trifoline

A Trifoline[b] vine, I am not, I confess, of the first vintage, but even so I shall be seventh among wines.[c]

115. Caecuban

Generous Caecuban[d] is ripened at Amyclae near Fundi. The green vine is born in the middle of the marsh.

116. Signine

Will you drink Signine, that checks loose bowels?[e] Lest you repress them too much, let your thirst be sparing.

[c] M. seems to imply the existence of a recognized classification, like that of comic poets by Volcatius Sedigitus (Morel, *Fragm. poet. Lat.*, p. 46). Possibly though he should be translated: "my vine shall be among the seventh (category of) wines."

[d] A stimulating and vigorous wine to be laid down: Athen. 27a (K).

[e] So Pliny *N.H.* 14.65, who speaks of its excessive dryness.

117 Mamertinum

Amphora Nestorea tibi Mamertina senecta
si detur, quodvis nomen habere potest.

118 Tarraconense

Tarraco, Campano tantum cessura Lyaeo,
haec genuit Latiis aemula vina cadis.

119 Nomentanum

Nomentana meum tibi dat vindemia Bacchum:
si te Quintus amat, commodiora bibes.

120 Spoletinum

De Spoletinis quae sunt cariosa lagonis
malueris quam si musta Falerna bibas.

121 Paelignum

Marsica Paeligni mittunt turbata coloni:
non tu, libertus sed bibat illa tuus.

118.2 Latiis *Gilbert* : tuscis Tβγ

---

[a] From Messana in Sicily. It was a sweet and light
wine: Athen. 27d.

[b] You can call it what you like, it will pass and the label
will be illegible; cf. 1.105.4.

[c] See Appendix A.

[d] Ovidius, M.'s neighbor at Nomentum. Nomentan
wine could be good when aged (1.105.4).

BOOK XIII

117. Mamertine

If a jar of Mamertine[a] as old as Nestor be given to you, it can bear any name you please.[b]

118. Tarragonese

Tarraco, that will yield only to the vintages of Campania, gave birth to these wines, which rival Latin[c] jars.

119. Nomentan

A Nomentan vintage gives you my wine. If Quintus[d] loves you, you will drink better.

120. Spoletine

You would prefer crusted wines from Spoletine flagons to drinking Falernian must.[e]

121. Paelignian

Paelignian growers send turbid Marsic.[f] Don't drink it yourself, but let your freedman do so.

---

[e] Spoletine was a poor wine (cf. 14.116), and it is no great tribute to say that when aged it was better than new Falernian. Athenaeus (27b) says it was sweet and golden in color.

[f] Very dry, and good for the stomach (Athen. 26f).

122 Acetum

Amphora Niliaci non sit tibi vilis aceti:
    esset cum vini, vilior illa fuit.

123 Massilitanum

Cum tua centenos expunget sportula civis,
    fumea Massiliae ponere vina potes.

124 Caeretanum

Caeretana Nepos ponat, Setina putabis.
    non ponit turbae, cum tribus illa bibit.

125 Tarentinum

Nobilis et lanis et felix vitibus Aulon
    det pretiosa tibi vellera, vina mihi.

126 Unguentum

Unguentum heredi numquam nec vina relinquas.
    ille habeat nummos, haec tibi tota dato.

122.2 uini γ : uinum αβ

---

[a] Egyptian vinegar was celebrated: Athen. 67c; Juv.
13.85. M. plays on two senses of *vilis*, "contemptible" and
"cheap."
[b] I.e. when you wish to repay clients for their services.
[c] Cf. 10.36.1.
[d] Cf. 6.27.1.

122. Vinegar

Don't despise a jar of Nile vinegar. When it was of wine, it was cheaper.[a]

123. Massilian

When your dole shall mark off a hundred citizens,[b] you can serve them smoky wines of Massilia.[c]

124. Caeretan

Let Nepos[d] serve Caeretan,[e] you will think it Setine. He does not serve it to a crowd, but drinks it with three guests.[f]

125. Tarentine

Let Aulon,[g] renowned for wool and blest in vines, give costly fleeces to you and wine[h] to me.

126. Unguent

Never leave unguent or wine to your heir. Let him have the money, but give these all to yourself

[e] From Caere in Etruria.

[f] He treats it with much respect.

[g] A valley near Tarentum; cf. Hor. *Od.* 2.6.18.

[h] Sweet, mild, and good for the stomach, but lacking "punch" (Athen. 27c).

MARTIAL

127 Coronae roseae

Dat festinatas, Caesar, tibi bruma coronas:
    quondam veris erat, nunc tua facta rosa est.

BOOK XIII

127. Garlands of roses

Winter gives you forced garlands, Caesar. The rose used to be spring's, now it has become yours.[a]

[a] Cf. 6.80.

[LIBER XIV]

APOPHORETA

1

Synthesibus dum gaudet eques dominusque senator
    dumque decent nostrum pillea sumpta Iovem;
nec timet aedilem moto spectare fritillo,
    cum videat gelidos tam prope verna lacus:
5 divitis alternas et pauperis accipe sortes:
    praemia convivae det sua quisque suo.
'sunt apinae tricaeque et si quid vilius istis.'
    quis nescit? vel quis tam manifesta negat?
sed quid agam potius madidis, Saturne, diebus,
10 quos tibi pro caelo filius ipse dedit?
vis scribam Thebas Troiamve malasve Mycenas?
    'lude' inquis 'nucibus': perdere nolo nuces.

1.6 det $\beta\gamma$: dent T

---

[a] Cf. 11.6.4n.
[b] Domitian.
[c] Lucian says (*Saturn.* 2) that a common Saturnalian joke was to blacken a man's face and to duck him in

226

BOOK XIV

APOPHORETA

1

While the knight and my lord senator rejoice in
dinner suits and the wearing of the cap of liberty[a]
befits our Jupiter,[b] while the slave as he shakes the
dice box does not fear to look at the aedile, though
he sees the cold pools so close:[c] accept these lots,
alternately for the rich man and the poor man; let
each one give his guest the appropriate prize.[d]
"They are trash and rubbish and anything worth
less than that, if possible." Who but knows it? Or
who denies anything so obvious? But what better
have I to do in your tipsy days, Saturn, which your
son[e] himself gave you in return for the sky? Do you
want me to write of Thebes or Troy or wicked
Mycenae? "Play with nuts," you say. But I don't
want to lose my nuts.[f]

the water (K). But the point here is obscure.

[d] See Intr. p. 2.

[e] Jupiter.

[f] Cf. 5.30.8.

2

Quo vis cumque loco potes hunc finire libellum:
  versibus explicitum est omne duobus opus.
lemmata si quaeris cur sint ascripta, docebo:
  ut, si malueris, lemmata sola legas.

3 Pugillares citrei

Secta nisi in tenues essemus ligna tabellas,
  essemus Libyci nobile dentis onus.

4 Quinquiplices

Caede iuvencorum domini calet area felix,
  quinquiplici cera cum datur altus honos.

5 Pugillares eborei

Languida ne tristes obscurent lumina cerae,
  nigra tibi niveum littera pingat ebur.

6 Triplices

Tunc triplices nostros non vilia dona putabis,
  cum se venturam scribet amica tibi.

2

You can finish this book at any place you choose.
Every performance is completed in two lines. If you
ask why headings are added, I'll tell you: so that, if
you prefer, you may read the headings only.

3. Tablets of citrus wood

If we had not been cut into thin tablets, we should
be the noble burden of a Libyan tusk.[a]

4. Five-leaved tablets

The happy forecourt of the master is warm with the
slaughter of steers when exalted honor is granted by
a five-leaved wax tablet.[b]

5. Ivory tablets

Lest somber wax dim your failing eyes, let black
letters paint snow-white ivory for your use.

6. Three-leaved tablets

You will think our three-leaved tablets no paltry
gift[c] when your mistress writes to you that she is
coming.

[a] Round tabletops (*orbes*) supported on ivory legs; cf.
9.59.7f.
[b] The sacrifice takes place when the tablets arrive by
which the Emperor sends notice of promotion.
[c] Generally so considered: cf. 7.72.2; 10.87.6.

MARTIAL

7 Pugillares membranei

Esse puta ceras, licet haec membrana vocetur:
delebis, quotiens scripta novare voles.

8 Vitelliani

Nondum legerit hos licet puella,
novit quid cupiant Vitelliani.

9 Idem

Quod minimos cernis, mitti nos credis amicae.
falleris: et nummos ista tabella rogat.

10 Chartae maiores

Non est munera quod putes pusilla,
cum donat vacuas poeta chartas.

11 Chartae epistulares

Seu leviter noto seu caro missa sodali
omnes ista solet charta vocare suos.

BOOK XIV

7. Parchment tablets

Suppose it wax, though it be called parchment. You will erase whenever you want to write afresh.[a]

8. Vitellian tablets

Although she may not have read them yet, a girl knows what Vitellian tablets[b] want.

9. The same

Because you see we are very small, you think we are being sent to somebody's mistress. You are wrong. This tablet asks for money also.

10. Bigger sheets

There's no reason for you to think it a petty present when a poet gives you blank sheets.[c]

11. Letter paper

Whether sent to a slight acquaintance or a dear friend, this paper calls everybody "dear."[d]

[a] The parchment seems to have been specially prepared so as to admit of erasure, as on a wax tablet (K).

[b] Of very small size, perhaps named after the maker. They were often used for billets-doux: cf. 2.6.6.

[c] Instead of poems.

[d] *Suus* was commonly used in the heading to a letter, e.g. *C. Plinius Maximo suo s. (salutem).*

12 Loculi eborei

Hos nisi de flava loculos implere moneta
non decet: argentum vilia ligna ferant.

13 Loculi lignei

Si quid adhuc superest in nostri faece locelli,
munus erit. nihil est; ipse locellus erit.

14 Tali eborei

Cum steterit nullus vultu tibi talus eodem,
munera me dices magna dedisse tibi.

15 Tesserae

Non sim talorum numero par tessera, dum sit
maior quam talis alea saepe mihi.

16 Turricula

Quae scit compositos manus improba mittere talos,
si per me misit, nil nisi vota facit.

16.2 facit $\beta\gamma$: ferret T : feret *Schneidewin*

---

[a] The *iactus Veneris*, or highest throw with the *tali*, was where each of them turned up a different number. The *tali* were four in number, and four flat sides were marked 1, 3, 4, and 6. The remaining two sides were rounded and blank.

[b] The plural *tessarae* would have been more appropriate, but meter forbade; cf. Ep. 17. Two, sometimes three, *tessarae* were used.

12. Ivory cashboxes

It is not proper to fill these boxes with anything except yellow money. Let cheap wood carry silver.

13. Wooden cashboxes

If anything still remains in the dregs of my cashbox, it will be a present. Is there nothing? The box itself shall be the present.

14. Ivory knucklebones

When none of the bones you throw stands with the same face as another, you will say that I have given you a big present.[a]

15. Dice

I am a die.[b] Let me not equal the knucklebones in number, provided the stakes are often higher for me than for them.[c]

16. Little tower

If the shameless hand that knows how to throw the bones prearranged has thrown them through me, it does nothing but pray.[d]

[c] Cf. 4.66.15.
[d] The *turricula* seems to have been grooved on the inside to prevent cheating. On the reading see *SB*[1].

17 Tabula lusoria

Hac mihi bis seno numeratur tessera puncto;
  calculus hac gemino discolor hoste perit.

18 (20) Calculi

Insidiosorum si ludis bella latronum,
  gemmeus iste tibi miles et hostis erit.

19 (18) Nuces

Alea parva nuces et non damnosa videtur;
  saepe tamen pueris abstulit illa natis.

20 (19) Theca libraria

Sortitus thecam calamis armare memento:
  cetera nos dedimus, tu leviora para.

---

[a] The epigram is on a gaming table suitable both for the game "of the twelve lines" (similar to backgammon) and the game of "robbers" (like chess or draughts): cf. 7.72.8. In the first game the highest throw appears to have been two sixes: cf. (of three dice) Aesch. *Ag.* 33. In the second

17. Gaming board[a]

On this side of me the die scores[b] with double sixes. On this other a piece of different color is killed by two foemen.

18 (20). Pieces

If you play the war game of stealthy mercenaries,[c] this glass fellow will be your soldier and your enemy.[d]

19 (18). Nuts

Nuts seem a small stake, one not ruinous; and yet that stake has often cost boys their buttocks.[e]

20 (19). Case for writing materials

Having drawn the case in the lottery, remember to equip it with pens. We have furnished the rest, you must provide the lesser items.

game a piece was taken by being hemmed in by two opposing "robbers"; cf. Ep. 20 (K; but see note c below).

[b] See on 4.29.7.

[c] Usually translated "robbers," but these pieces are also called "soldiers" (*milites*) here and in *Laus Pis.* 193 and 207, and *latro* meant "mercenary soldier" in early Latin.

[d] Or "this glass soldier will also be your enemy," i.e. in the next game he may be on the other side.

[e] I.e. earned them a flogging; cf. 5.84.1f. But Gronovius may have been right to suspect sens. obsc. For the verb cf. Ov. *Met.* 7.348 *plura locuturo cum verbis guttura Colchis / abstulit* ("cut his throat").

21 Graphiarium

Haec tibi erunt armata suo graphiaria ferro:
  si puero dones, non leve munus erit.

22 Dentiscalpium

Lentiscum melius: sed si tibi frondea cuspis
  defuerit, dentes pinna levare potest.

23 Auriscalpium

Si tibi morosa prurigine verminat auris,
  arma damus tantis apta libidinibus.

24 Acus aurea

Splendida ne madidi violent bombycina crines,
  figat acus tortas sustineatque comas.

25 Pectines

Quid faciet nullos hic inventura capillos
  multifido buxus quae tibi dente datur?

26 Crines

Chattica Teutonicos accendit spuma capillos:
  captivis poteris cultior esse comis.

---

a For writing on wax.

b "A twig from the leafy mastic tree" (*OLD*).

c *Libidinibus* alludes to a different kind of *prurigo,*
arma to the sense mentioned in *TLL* II.601.58 (*SB*[1]).

21. Stilus case

These stilus cases you will arm with their steel.[a] If you give them to a boy, it will be no slight gift.

22. Toothpick

Mastic is better; but if a leafy point[b] is not available, a quill can relieve your teeth.

23. Earpick

If your ear is plagued by a capricious itch, I give you a weapon apt to such urges.[c]

24. Gold pin

Lest damp hair harm bright silks, let a pin fix and hold up the twisted locks.

25. Combs

This present of boxwood with multifissured tooth will find no hair here. What will it be good for?

26. Hair

Chattian foam lights up Teutonic locks. You can be smarter with captive hair.[d]

[d] Ladies wore false hair, much of which came from Germany, or from German captives. This hair was dyed with *sapo*, consisting of goats' fat and beechwood ashes (Pliny *N.H.* 28.191) in the form of balls. See next epigram and cf. *spuma Batava* in 8.33.20 (K).

27 Sapo

Si mutare paras longaevos cana capillos,
    accipe Mattiacas — quo tibi calva? — pilas.

28 Umbella

Accipe quae nimios vincant umbracula soles:
    sit licet et ventus, te tua vela tegent.

29 Causea

In Pompeiano tecum spectabo theatro.
    nam flatus populo vela negare solet.

30 Venabula

Excipient apros expectabuntque leones,
    intrabunt ursos, sit modo firma manus.

31 Culter venatorius

Si deiecta gemas longo venabula rostro,
    hic brevis ingentem comminus ibit aprum.

29.2 nam flatus *Pontanus* : nam ventus γ : mandatus Tβ

BOOK XIV

27. Hair dye

If you wish to change your superannuated hair, white-headed lady, accept balls from the Mattiaci.[a] Why go bald?

28. Sunshade

Accept a sunshade to defeat the fierce sun. Should there be wind too,[b] your own awning will cover you.

29. Broad-brimmed hat

I shall be a spectator with you in Pompey's theater. For the wind is apt to deny the people an awning.[c]

30. Hunting spears

They will receive boars and await lions, they will enter bears, only provided the hand be firm.

31. Hunting knife

If you groan that your hunting spear with its long blade has been dropped, this short knife will tackle a huge boar at close quarters.

[a] Tribe of the Chatti in the area of Wiesbaden. Or perhaps "from Mattium," their settlement.
[b] When the ordinary *vela* could not be spread or had to be furled: cf. 14.29.2.
[c] Therefore the head requires a covering. The *causea* was a high-crowned and broad-brimmed hat. It came originally from Macedonia: Val. Max. 5.1[ext.].4, and was especially worn by fishermen and sailors (K).

32 Parazonium

Militiae decus hoc gratique erit omen honoris,
    arma tribunicium cingere digna latus.

33 Pugio

Pugio, quem curva signat brevis orbita vena,
    stridentem gelidis hunc Salo tinxit aquis.

34 Falx

Pax me certa ducis placidos curvavit in usus.
    agricolae nunc sum, militis ante fui.

35 Securicula

Cum fieret tristis solvendis auctio nummis,
    haec quadringentis milibus empta fuit.

36 Ferramenta tonsoria

Tondendis haec arma tibi sunt apta capillis;
    unguibus hic longis utilis, illa genis.

---

[a] The *parazonium* was a waist belt carrying a sword worn on the left side by military tribunes, whereas the ordinary soldier wore his sword slung on the right side by a shoulder strap (K).

[b] A stamp.

[c] Cf. 1.49.12.

[d] A converted sword.

32. Belt and sword[a]

A soldier's distinction this will be and an omen of a welcome honor, arms worthy to gird the side of a tribune.

33. Dagger

A dagger, which a narrow circle[b] marks with curving groove: this did Salo[c] dip hissing in his icy waters.

34. Sickle[d]

Our Leader's assured peace curved me for quiet employments. I am now the farmer's, I used to be the soldier's.

35. Small hatchet

When a dismal auction was held for payment of debts, this was bought for four hundred thousand.[e]

36. Barber's metal gear

This implement[f] is useful for cutting your hair, this[g] is apt for long nails, that[h] for your cheeks.

[e] The price is meant to be absurd. The *securicula* was a child's ornament or toy: cf. Plaut. *Rud.* 1159. Such things were also hung round children's necks as amulets, or as proofs of identity (K).
[f] Scissors.
[g] Little knife.
[h] Razor.

37 Scrinium

Constrictos nisi das mihi libellos,
admittam tineas trucesque blattas.

38 Fasces calamorum

Dat chartis habiles calamos Memphitica tellus;
texantur reliqua tecta palude tibi.

39 Lucerna cubicularis

Dulcis conscia lectuli lucerna,
quidquid vis facias licet, tacebo.

40 Cicindela

Ancillam tibi sors dedit lucernae,
totas quae vigil exigit tenebras.

41 Lucerna polymyxos

Illustrem cum tota meis convivia flammis
totque geram myxos, una lucerna vocor.

37.1 constrictos $\beta\gamma$: selectos T

---

[a] The *scrinium* was a cylindrical case for holding books
and papers.
[b] Properly "glowworm" (*cicindela*).

37. Bookcase[a]

Unless you give me books packed tight, I shall admit moths and savage bookworms.

38. Bundles of pens

The land of Memphis gives reeds handy for writing. With reeds from other swamps let your roof be thatched.

39. Bedroom lamp

I am a lamp, confidante of your sweet bed. You may do whatever you will, I shall be silent.

40. Candle[b]

The lot has given you a handmaid to your lamp.[c] She keeps awake all through the hours of darkness.

41. Lamp with many wicks

Although I light up whole dinner parties with my flames and bear so many wicks, I am called one lamp.[d]

---

[c] Candles were made of rope or rush dipped in wax, tallow, or pitch. A candle was a poor man's light; hence it is called a "handmaid" of the rich man's lamp; cf. Juv. 3.287 (K).

[d] Lamps with even fourteen wicks have been found at Pompeii and Herculaneum (K).

MARTIAL

42 Cereus

Hic tibi nocturnos praestabit cereus ignis:
subducta est puero namque lucerna tuo.

43 Candelabrum Corinthium

Nomina candelae nobis antiqua dederunt.
non norat parcos uncta lucerna patres.

44 Candelabrum ligneum

Esse vides lignum; servas nisi lumina, fiet
de candelabro magna lucerna tibi.

45 Pila paganica

Haec quae de facili turget paganica pluma,
folle minus laxa est et minus arta pila.

46 Pila trigonalis

Si me mobilibus scis expulsare sinistris,
sum tua. si nescis, rustice, redde pilam.

45.1 de facili *scripsi* : difficili Tβ : -lis γ   46.1 mobilibus *Scaliger* : no- Tβγ   46.2 tu (T) nescis? *edd.*

---

[a] Mingling gold, silver, and copper. According to Pliny (*N.H.* 34.8), there were three types of "Corinthian" bronze, silver predominating in the first, gold in the second, while in the third the three metals were in equal proportions.

42. Wax taper

This taper will afford you light at night; for the lamp has been stolen from your boy.

43. Corinthian[a] candelabrum

Candles gave me my ancient name. The oil lamp knew not our thrifty sires.

44. Wooden candelabrum

You see I am wood. Unless you watch the light, your candelabrum will turn into a great lamp.[b]

45. Paganica (ball)

This paganica that swells with yielding feathers is not so soft as the follis and not so hard as the handball.[c]

46. Triangle ball

If you know how to drive me off with nimble left-handers,[d] I am yours. If you don't, clod, return the ball.[e]

[b] The wood will catch fire.

[c] As to the balls mentioned in this and the three following epigrams, cf. 4.19.5f and 7.32.7.

[d] Cf. 7.72.11.

[e] A technical term in the game? But here and in 163 with the sense "give up playing."

47 Follis

Ite procul, iuvenes: mitis mihi convenit aetas:
    folle decet pueros ludere, folle senes.

48 Harpasta

Haec rapit Antaei velox in pulvere draucus,
    grandia qui vano colla labore facit.

49 Halteres

Quid pereunt stulto fortes haltere lacerti?
    exercet melius vinea fossa viros.

50 Galericulum

Ne lutet immundum nitidos ceroma capillos,
    hac poteris madidas condere pelle comas.

51 Strigiles

Pergamon has misit. curvo destringere ferro:
    non tam saepe teret lintea fullo tibi.

52 Gutus corneus

Gestavit modo fronte me iuvencus:
    verum rhinocerota me putabis.

52.2 putabis β : -bas γ : -bat T

---

[a] Because unproductive.
[b] I.e. on the athletic ground. The development of a
short, muscular neck was aimed at by athletes: Juv. 3.88;

47. Follis

Go away, young fellows. A gentle age suits me. The follis is for boys to play with, likewise old men.

48. Harpasta (ball)

These the swift athlete, who makes his neck big by futile[a] toil, snatches in Antaeus' dust.[b]

49. Dumbbells

Why do stout arms go to waste on the silly dumbbell? Digging a vineyard is better exercise for men.

50. Leather cap

Lest the dirty wrestlers' mud soil your sleek locks, you can hide your damp hair with this skin.

51. Skin-scrapers

Pergamum sent these. Scrape yourself with the curved blade. The fuller will not so often wear out your towels.[c]

52. Horn oil flask

A steer bore me lately on his forehead. You will think me genuine rhinoceros.[d]

and see Pliny *N.H.* 14.140 (*pectorosa cervicis repandae ostentatio*) (K).

[c] They will not need cleaning so often.

[d] Oil flasks of rhinoceros horn were used at the baths by the rich: Juv. 7.130.

53 Rhinoceros

Nuper in Ausonia domini spectatus harena
  hic erit ille tibi cui pila taurus erat.

54 Crepitaculum

Si quis plorator collo tibi vernula pendet,
  haec quatiat tenera garrula sistra manu.

55 Flagellum

Proficies nihil hoc, caedas licet usque, flagello,
  si tibi purpureo e grege currit equus.

56 Dentifricium

Quid mecum est tibi? me puella sumat:
  emptos non soleo polire dentes.

57 Myrobalanum

Quod nec Vergilius nec carmine dicit Homerus,
  hoc ex unguento constat et ex balano.

53.2 hic erit ille tibi $\beta\gamma$: hic erat ille dies T

---

[a] Perhaps the title should be *Idem* ("The same"), in which case the flask is bull's horn but taken by the recipient for rhinocerus horn, as in the previous epigram. Otherwise we may think of a toy rhinoceros. See *SB*[1].

[b] Cf. Sp. 11.4; 10.86.4.

[c] It, and the Gold, had been added by Domitian (Suet. *Dom.* 7.1). Friedländer suggests that they had somehow incurred his displeasure and been abolished.

53. Rhinoceros[a]

This to you will be he that was lately in our Lord's Ausonian arena, to whom a bull was as a straw dummy.[b]

54. Small rattle

If a little home-born slave hang weeping from your neck, let him shake this chattering rattle with his tender hand.

55. Whip

You will make no headway with this whip, though you lay it on continually, if the horse that runs for you be of the purple persuasion.[c]

56. Dentifrice

What have you[d] to do with me? Let a girl take me. I am not in the habit of polishing purchased teeth.

57. Ben nut[e]

This, which neither Virgil nor Homer mentions in his poems, consists of unguent and ben nut.

---

[d] An old woman.

[e] The word would not go into the metre. *Myrobalanum* is described by Pliny (*N.H.* 12.100–103) as the fruit of a tree found in the Thebais and in Arabia with a leaf like that of a heliotrope, the fruit being of the size of a filbert. From it was extracted an oil used in compounding unguent. Cf. also Pliny, 13.18; 23.98. The modern name of the tree is *Moringa oleifera* (K).

58 Aphronitrum

Rusticus es, nescis quid Graeco nomine dicar:
spuma vocor nitri. Graecus es: aphronitrum.

59 Opobalsama

Balsama me capiunt, haec sunt unguenta virorum:
delicias Cosmi vos redolete, nurus.

60 Lomentum

Gratum munus erit scisso nec inutile ventri,
si clara Stephani balnea luce petes.

61 Lanterna cornea

Dux lanterna viae clusis feror aurea flammis,
et tuta est gremio parva lucerna meo.

62 Lanterna de vesica

Cornea si non sum, numquid sum fuscior? aut me
vesicam, contra qui venit, esse putat?

58.2 ἀφρόνιτρον *coni. Lindsay*

---

a *Spuma nitri* was prized, and prescribed by doctors in
pills or pastilles: Pliny *N.H.* 31.112 seq.; and balls of it
were given as presents: Stat. *Silv.* 4.9.37. It was found in
Asia in caves called *colycae* as a distillation from the rock
and was afterwards dried in the sun. The best was
Lydian: Pliny *ibid.* (K).

b The juice of the balsam tree; called balm of Gilead or
of Mecca, and found, according to Pliny, only in Judaea. It
appears to have become known in Rome in the time of

58. Saltpetre

You are a peasant, you don't know my Greek name:
I'm called froth of nitre.[a] You are a Greek: aphroni-
trum.

59. Opobalsam[b]

Balsam for me! This is the perfume for men.[c] Smell
of Cosmus' favorites, you young wives.

60. Bean meal[d]

This will be a welcome gift, not useless to a fissured
stomach if you go to Stephanus' baths in broad day-
light.

61. Horn lantern

A golden lantern, guide of your way, I am carried
with my flame enclosed, and a small lamp is safe in
my bosom.

62. Lantern made of bladder

If I am not made of horn, am I any the dimmer? Or
does he who meets me think I am bladder?

Pompey, who displayed the tree in one of his triumphs.
See Pliny *N.H.* 12.111–123; 13.8, 11, 13, 15, 18; 15.30;
23.92 (K).

[c] Juv. (2.41) seems to have been of a different opinion
(K).

[d] Cf. 3.42.1.

63 (64) Tibiae

Ebria nos madidis rumpit tibicina buccis:
    saepe duas pariter, saepe monaulon habet.

64 (63) Fistula

Quid me compactam ceris et harundine rides?
    quae primum structa est fistula talis erat.

65 Soleae lanatae

Defuerit si forte puer soleasque libebit
    sumere, pro puero pes erit ipse sibi.

66 Mamillare

Taurino poteras pectus constringere tergo:
    nam pellis mammas non capit ista tuas.

67 Muscarium pavoninum

Lambere quae turpes prohibet tua prandia muscas,
    alitis eximiae cauda superba fuit.

68 (71) Muscarium bubulum

Sordida si flavo fuerit tibi pulvere vestis,
    colligat hunc tenui verbere cauda levis.

---

[a] Single pipe. Two pipes were sometimes played, and they were *pares* or *impares*, the former being of the same length, the latter of unequal length. The right-hand pipe was the bass or manly pipe, the left-hand one the treble or womanly pipe (K).

[b] By the god Pan: cf. Virg. *Ecl.* 2.32.

63 (64). Pipes

The tipsy pipe girl bursts us with her madid cheeks.
Often she has two of us together, often she has a
monaulos.[a]

64 (63). Shepherd's pipe

Why do you laugh at me, compact as I am of wax
and reed? The first pipe ever made[b] was like me.

65. Wool-lined slippers

If by chance there's no slave to hand and you want
to put your slippers on, your foot will be its own
slave.[c]

66. Breast-band

You might have constrained your bosom "with a
bull's hide."[d] For this skin is not large enough for
your breasts.

67. Peacock-feather fly whisk

This that forbids nasty flies to lick your lunch was
the proud tail of a peerless bird.

68 (71). Ox-tail fly swat

If your clothes are soiled with yellow dust, let the
light tail collect it with a little flap.

[c] I.e. you can put your feet in the slippers without using
your hands.

[d] An allusion to Virg. *Aen.* 1.368 (*taurino quantum pos-
sent circumdare tergo*).

69 (68) Copta Rhodiaca

Peccantis famuli pugno ne percute dentes:
   clara Rhodos coptam quam tibi misit edat.

70 (69) Priapus siligineus

Si vis esse satur, nostrum potes esse Priapum;
   ipsa licet rodas inguina, purus eris.

71 (70) Porcus

Iste tibi faciet bona Saturnalia porcus,
   inter spumantes ilice pastus apros.

72 Botulus

Qui venit botulus mediae tibi tempore brumae,
   Saturni septem venerat ante dies.

73 Psittacus

Psittacus a vobis aliorum nomina discam.
   hoc didici per me dicere: 'Caesar have.'

74 Corvus

Corve salutator, quare fellator haberis?
   in caput intravit mentula nulla tuum.

---

[a] The Rhodian biscuit was very hard. There may be also a play upon the name *copta* and the Greek κόπτειν koptein (to beat) (K).

[b] I.e. this is *not* a passed-on Saturnalian present. Elsewhere M. writes of the holiday as lasting five days; under the Republic it lasted seven.

254

69 (68). Rhodian hardbake

Don't bash your delinquent servant's teeth with your fist; let him eat the hardbake sent you by famous Rhodes.[a]

70 (69). Priapus made of flour

If you want a full stomach, you can eat our Priapus; though you gnaw his very genitals, you will be clean.

71 (70). Pig

This pig will make you a good Saturnalia; he fed on acorns among the foaming boars.

72. Sausage

This sausage that has reached you at midwinter time had reached me before Saturn's seven days.[b]

73. Parrot

A parrot, I shall learn from you the names of others; this I have learned to say by myself: "Caesar, hail!"

74. Crow

Crow, who greet us, why are you thought to be a sucker? No cock has entered your head.[c]

[c] Cf. Pliny *N.H.* 10.15 *ore eos parere aut coire vulgus arbitratur . . . Aristoteles negat . . . sed illam osculationem quae saepe cernitur qualem in columbis esse*; Arist. *Gen. Anim.* 3.6.

75 Luscinia

Flet Philomela nefas incesti Tereos, et quae
   muta puella fuit, garrula fertur avis.

76 Pica

Pica loquax certa dominum te voce saluto:
   si me non videas, esse negabis avem.

77 Cavea eborea

Si tibi talis erit qualem dilecta Catullo
   Lesbia plorabat, hic habitare potest.

78 Narthecium

Artis ebur medicae narthecia cernis: habebis
   munera quae cuperet Paccius esse sua.

79 Flagra

Ludite lascivi, sed tantum ludite, servi.
   haec signata mihi quinque diebus erunt.

80 Ferulae

Invisae nimium pueris grataeque magistris,
   clara Prometheo munere ligna sumus.

---

[a] The sparrow of Catull. 2 and 3.

[b] The *narthecium* was, as its name implies, made in the
shape of a joint of the giant fennel (νάρθηξ) (K).

[c] See index.

[d] Slaves during the Saturnalia were allowed a degree of
license.

75. Nightingale

Philomela bewails the crime of foul Tereus, and she that was mute when a girl is called garrulous as a bird.

76. Magpie

A chattering magpie, I greet you as "lord" with a clear voice. If you did not see me, you would say I am no bird.

77. Ivory cage

If you have such a one as Lesbia, Catullus' beloved, mourned,[a] it can live here.

78. Medicine chest

You see a medicine chest,[b] ivory appanage of the healing art. You will have a gift which Paccius[c] would wish his own.

79. Whips

Play, frisky slaves, do nought but play.[d] These I shall keep under seal for five days.

80. Rods

Most hateful to boys and agreeable to school-masters, we are the sticks made famous by Prometheus' gift.[e]

[e] Prometheus, according to the myth, brought fire from Heaven in the stem of the giant fennel (*ferula* or *νάρθηξ*), and gave it to men (K).

81 Pera

Ne mendica ferat barbati prandia nudi
  dormiat et tetrico cum cane, pera rogat.

82 Scopae

In pretio scopas testatur palma fuisse.
  otia sed scopis nunc analecta dedit.

83 Scalptorium eboreum

Defendet manus haec scapulas mordente molesto
  pulice, vel si quid pulice sordidius.

84 Manuale

Ne toga barbatos faciat vel paenula libros,
  haec abies chartis tempora longa dabit.

85 Lectus pavoninus

Nomina dat spondae pictis pulcherrima pinnis
  nunc Iunonis avis, sed prius Argus erat.

81.2 tetrico γ : tristi Tβ 82.2 dedit T : dabunt $\beta\gamma$:
dabit *Scriverius*

---

[a] Used as a pillow. The Cynics, in imitation of beggars, equipped themselves with a staff and wallet: cf. 4.53.3 (K).
[b] It seems that the *analecta* (cf. 7.20.17) used only his hands.

81. Wallet

The wallet asks that it carry not the beggarly lunch
of a half-naked bearded one nor sleep with a sour
Cynic.[a]

82. Brooms

The palm attests that brooms were once valued, but
now the crumb collector has given brooms a rest.[b]

83. Ivory scratcher[c]

When a troublesome flea or anything nastier than a
flea bites your shoulder blades, this hand will
defend them.

84. Book holder

Lest gown or overcoat make your books bearded,[d]
this fir-wood will give long life to the paper.

85. Peacock couch

A bird, most beauteous with his painted plumage,
gives his name to a couch.[e] Now he is Juno's bird,
but formerly he was Argus.[f]

[c] It was in the shape of a hand.

[d] I.e. fray the edges of the rolls.

[e] From the veins in the wood (Pliny *N.H.* 13.96). Cf.
14.89n.

[f] See index.

86 Ephippium

Stragula succincti venator sume veredi:
nam solet a nudo surgere ficus equo.

87 Stibadia

Accipe lunata scriptum testudine sigma.
octo capit; veniat quisquis amicus erit.

88 Gustatorium

Femineam nobis cherson si credis inesse,
deciperis: pelagi mascula praeda sumus.

89 Mensa citrea

Accipe felices, Atlantica munera, silvas:
aurea qui dederit dona, minora dabit.

90 Mensa acerna

Non sum crispa quidem nec silvae filia Maurae,
sed norunt lautas et mea ligna dapes.

87.1 sigma ς : signa γ : ligna β

---

[a] *Veredus*, a fast breed of horse. The word is Celtic.
[b] Cf. 10.48.6n.
[c] Shell from the sea tortoise (? turtle) was held superior to that of the land tortoise, and the male shell was superior to the female. According to Pliny (*N.H.* 9.38) the land tortoises were called *chersinae* and were found in African deserts, where they subsisted on dew (K).

86. Saddlecloth

Take, huntsman, the cloth of a girt-up hunter;[a] for a fig is apt to arise from a bare-backed horse.

87. Semicircular couches

Accept a sigma[b] inlaid with crescent tortoiseshell. It takes eight. Let him come, whoever is a friend.

88. Tray for hors d'oeuvres

If you think a female land tortoise is part of me, you are deceived. I am male spoil of the sea.[c]

89. Citrus table[d]

Receive the fertile forests, gifts of Atlas. Who gives golden gifts, will give less.

90. Maple table

I am not veined, it is true, nor the daughter of a Moorish forest,[e] but my timber too knows luxurious repasts.

---

[d] The *citrus* (the tree called thyine wood, *Callitris quadrivalvis*, the Greek θύα or θύον) came from Mauretania, in northwest Africa: Pliny *N.H.* 13.96 *seqq.* Round tabletops (*orbes*) were made of it, for which incredible sums were often paid (K).

[e] I.e. neither veined (a feature greatly valued: Pliny *loc. cit.*) nor *citrus*. Maple was second to *citrus*: Pliny *N.H.* 16.66 *seqq.*; and one species was also peacock-veined: *ibid.* (K).

91 Dentes eborei

Grandia taurorum portant qui corpora, quaeris
   an Libycas possint sustinuisse trabes?

92 Quinquepedal

Puncta notis ilex et acuta cuspide clusa
   saepe redemptoris prodere furta solet.

93 Pocula archetypa

Non est ista recens, nec nostri gloria caeli:
   primus in his Mentor, dum facit illa, bibit.

94 Calices audaces

Nos sumus audacis plebeia toreumata vitri,
   nostra neque ardenti gemma feritur aqua.

95 Phiala aurea caelata

Quamvis Callaico rubeam generosa metallo,
   glorior arte magis: nam Myos iste labor.

96 Calices Vatinii

Vilia sutoris calicem monimenta Vatini
   accipe; sed nasus longior ille fuit.

---

[a] Cf. Sp. 18 and 20.
[b] Cf. 12.74.3n. On *toreumata* see 12.74.5n. *Vitri* seems
to be ironical, the cups being earthenware.
[c] Cf. 10.3.4n.

91. Ivory tusks

They can carry the great bodies of bulls;[a] do you ask whether they can support Libyan tabletops?

92. Five-foot rule

A piece of oak pricked with marks and ending in a sharp point is wont often to reveal a contractor's frauds.

93. Antique cups

Not of recent origin nor of Roman chisel is this glory. Mentor was first to drink from these cups while he was making them.

94. Bold cups

We are plebeian cups of bold[b] glass, and our ware is not cracked by hot water.

95. A chased gold bowl

Although I am noble and ruddy with Galician metal, I glory more in my workmanship, for this is the work of Mys.

96. Vatinian cups

Accept a cup, a cheap memorial of cobbler Vatinius;[c] but *that* nose was longer.

97 Lances chrysendetae

Grandia ne viola parvo chrysendeta mullo:
  ut minimum, libras debet habere duas.

98 Vasa Arretina

Arretina nimis ne spernas vasa monemus:
  lautus erat Tuscis Porsena fictilibus.

99 Bascauda

Barbara de pictis veni bascauda Britannis,
  sed me iam mavult dicere Roma suam.

100 Panaca

Si non ignota est docti tibi terra Catulli,
  potasti testa Raetica vina mea.

101 Boletaria

Cum mihi boleti dederint tam nobile nomen,
  prototomis — pudet heu! — servio coliculis.

102 Calices Surrentini

Accipe non vili calices de pulvere natos,
  sed Surrentinae leve toreuma rotae.

97.1 uiola *γ* : -le *β* : -les *Heinsius*

---

[a] See 1.53.6n.
[b] Nothing further is known, nor is it clear why these wines should have been drunk in Verona.

97. Gold-inlaid dishes

Do not insult large gold-inlaid dishes with a small mullet. At the least he ought to weigh two pounds.

98. Arretine ware

I advise you not to be too scornful of Arretine ware.[a] Porsenna was luxurious with Tuscan crockery.

99. Basket

I have come, a barbarian basket, from the painted Britons, but Rome now prefers to call me hers.

100. Panaca

If the country of poet Catullus is not unknown to you, you have drunk Rhaetian wines in my jar.[b]

101. Mushroom pots

Although mushrooms gave me so noble a name, I cater (I am deeply ashamed to say) to early sprouts.

102. Surrentine wine cups

Accept cups not born of common clay, but smooth shapings[c] of a Surrentine wheel.[d]

[c] Cf. 12.74.5n.
[d] Pliny classes Surrentine earthenware cups for excellence with those from Asta and Pollentia, and from Saguntum in Spain: *N.H.* 35.160 (K).

103 Colum nivarium

Setinos, moneo, nostra nive frange trientes:
　　pauperiore mero tingere lina potes.

104 Saccus nivarius

Attenuare nives norunt et lintea nostra:
　　frigidior colo non salit unda tuo.

105 Urceoli ministratorii

Frigida non deerit, non deerit calda petenti.
　　sed tu morosa ludere parce siti.

106 Urceus fictilis

Hic tibi donatur panda ruber urceus ansa.
　　Stoicus hoc gelidam Fronto petebat aquam.

107 Calathi

Nos Satyri, nos Bacchus amat, nos ebria tigris,
　　perfusos domini lambere docta pedes.

106.1 panda ς : pansa γ : laxa β

103. Strainer for snow[a]

Take my advice, dilute your Setine cups with my snow. You can stain linen with an inferior wine.

104. Bag for straining through snow

My linen also knows how to reduce snow: no colder spurts the water from your strainer.

105. Small jugs for table service

Cold water will not be lacking, nor warm either, when you ask for it. But forbear to dally with a pernickety thirst.[b]

106. Earthenware jug

This red jug with arched handle[c] is presented to you. With this Fronto the Stoic used to ask for cold water.

107. Goblets[d]

The Satyrs love us, Bacchus loves us, and so does the tipsy tigress that has been taught to lick her master's[e] wine-drenched feet.

[a] Cf. 5.64. The *colum nivarium* was a metal colander in which a lump of frozen snow was placed, and the wine was strained through it into the cup or other wine vessel (K).

[b] I.e. do not be fussy about the precise temperature.

[c] Cf. *OLD pandus* "of things with downward turned extremities."

[d] Cups or jugs called *calathi* ("baskets").

[e] Bacchus.

108 Calices Saguntini

Quae non sollicitus teneat servetque minister
sume Saguntino pocula facta luto.

109 Calices gemmati

Gemmatum Scythicis ut luceat ignibus aurum
aspice. quot digitos exuit iste calix!

110 Ampulla potoria

Hac licet in gemma, servat quae nomina Cosmi,
luxuriose, bibas, si foliata sitis.

111 Crystallina

Frangere dum metuis, franges crystallina: peccant
securae nimium sollicitaeque manus.

112 Nimbus vitreus

A Iove qui veniet, miscenda ad pocula largas
fundet nimbus aquas: hic tibi vina dabit.

113 Murrina

Si caldum potas, ardenti murra Falerno
convenit et melior fit sapor inde mero.

---

[a] M. speaks disparagingly of Saguntine clayware; cf.
8.6.2; Pliny praises it, at least for cups: *N.H.* 35.160 (K).

[b] Rich men often ornamented their cups with jewels
from their finger rings: cf. Juv. 5.43.

[c] On *foliatum* see 11.27.9n. The flask had formerly con-
tained this perfume and would flavor the wine. Perfumes

108. Saguntine cups

Take cups made of Saguntan clay which your servant may hold and keep without anxiety.[a]

109. Jewelled cups

See how the jewelled gold is alight with Scythian fires. How many fingers has this cup despoiled![b]

110. Drinking flask

Luxury-lover, you may drink in this jewelled flask that keeps the name of Cosmus, if you thirst for perfumed wine.[c]

111. Crystal

So long as you are afraid of breaking crystal cups, break them you will. Hands too careless and too anxious alike do amiss.

112. Glass shower

The shower that comes from Jove will pour water in plenty to mix your cups. This one will give you wine.[d]

113. Murrines

If you drink it hot, the murrine suits the ardent Falernian and gives the wine a better flavor.

were actually mixed with wine; see Friedländer on Juv. 6.303.

[d] *Nimbus* (rain cloud or shower) is evidently a device for sprinkling wine.

114 Patella Cumana

Hanc tibi Cumano rubicundam pulvere testam
municipem misit casta Sibylla suam.

115 Calices vitrei

Aspicis ingenium Nili: quibus addere plura
dum cupit, ah quotiens perdidit auctor opus!

116 Lagona nivaria

Spoletina bibis vel Marsis condita cellis:
quo tibi decoctae nobile frigus aquae?

117 Idem

Non potare nivem sed aquam potare recentem
de nive commenta est ingeniosa sitis.

118 Idem

Massiliae fumos miscere nivalibus undis
parce, puer, constet ne mihi pluris aqua.

118.2 mihi *scripsi* : tibi Tβγ

BOOK XIV

114. Cuman dish

The chaste Sibyl[a] has sent you this platter red with Cuman earth, her fellow townsman.

115. Glass cups

You see the ingenuity of Nile. Desiring to add more to them, ah, how often has the artist spoiled his work![b]

116. Flagon for snow

You drink Spoletine or wine laid down in Marsian cellars.[c] What use to you is the noble chill of iced water?[d]

117. Same

Ingenious thirst has invented a way of not drinking snow but drinking water fresh from snow.[e]

118. Same

Forbear, boy, to mix Massilia's smoke[f] with snow water, lest the water cost me[g] more than the wine.

[a] Cf. 9.29.3.
[b] I.e. the ornamented cups.
[c] These wines were inferior; cf. 13.120 and 121.
[d] *Decocta* (as to which cf. 2.85.1) is wasted on them.
[e] Cf. 5.64.2.
[f] Cf. 10.36.1; 13.123.2.
[g] "You" (*tibi*) in the manuscripts, but the slave would not be paying.

271

119 Matella fictilis

Dum poscor crepitu digitorum et verna moratur,
  o quotiens paelex culcita facta mea est!

120 Ligula argentea

Quamvis me ligulam dicant equitesque patresque,
  dicor ab indoctis lingula grammaticis.

121 Coclearia

Sum cocleis habilis sed nec minus utilis ovis.
  numquid scis, potius cur cocleare vocer?

122 Anuli

ante frequens sed nunc rarus nos donat amicus.
  felix cui comes est non alienus eques.

123 Dactyliotheca

Saepe gravis digitis elabitur anulus unctis,
  tuta mea fiet sed tua gemma fide.

---

[a] The learning which makes them offend against common usage is as bad as ignorance. *Lingula* ("little tongue") is etymologically correct.

BOOK XIV

119. Earthenware chamberpot

While I am summoned with a snap of the fingers and the slave delays, oh, how often has a pillow become my rival!

120. Silver spoon

Though knights and senators call me *ligula*, I am called *lingula* by ignorant grammarians.[a]

121. Snail spoon

I am convenient for snails, but no less useful for eggs. Do you know why I am rather called a snail spoon?[b]

122. Rings

In time past friends often gave us as presents, but nowadays it rarely happens. Happy is he whose escort is a knight of his own making.[c]

123. Ring case

A heavy ring often slips from greasy fingers, but your gem will find safety in my trust.

[b] The *cocleare* was a spoon with a point at one end, and smaller (8.71.9f) than the *ligula*. The point was used to pick snails (*cocleae*) or shellfish out of their shells; hence the name. Petr. 33 speaks of *coclearia* of "not less than half a pound" weight used for eating eggs, but then they were Trimalchio's spoons (K).

[c] Whose qualification he has supplied (cf. 5.19.10). The ring was the mark of a knight: cf. 8.5.2.

124 Toga

Romanos rerum dominos gentemque togatam
ille facit, magno qui dedit astra patri.

125 Idem

Si matutinos facile est tibi perdere somnos,
attrita veniet sportula saepe toga.

126 Endromis

Pauperis est munus sed non est pauperis usus:
hanc tibi pro laena mittimus endromida.

127 Canusinae fuscae

Haec tibi turbato Canusina simillima mulso
munus erit. gaude: non cito fiet anus.

128 Bardocucullus

Gallia Santonico vestit te bardocucullo.
cercopithecorum paenula nuper erat.

125.1 perdere Tγ : rumpere β

---

[a] Domitian, who founded a temple to the Flavian family
(cf. 9.1.8). He seems to have enjoined the use of the toga in
certain public places; cf. Suet. *Aug.* 40.5.

[b] From Virg. *Aen.* 1.282.

[c] The *endromis* was not a garment, but a warm wrapper
of rough texture used by richer men for warmth after gym-
nastic exercises: cf. 4.19.

124. Gown (toga)

He that gave the stars to his great father[a] makes "the Romans lords of the world and people of the gown."[b]

125. Same

If you don't mind losing your morning sleep, you will wear out your gown and often get a dole.

126. Thick wrap

A poor man's gift it is, but not a poor man's wear. This wrap I send you in lieu of a cloak.[c]

127. Brown Canusian cloak

This Canusian cloak, very like in color to turbid mead,[d] shall be your gift. Be happy; it will not soon grow old.

128. Hooded overcoat

Gaul clothes you in a Santonian hooded overcoat.[e] Recently it was the coat of long-tailed monkeys.[f]

[d] Cf. 9.22.9n.

[e] Cf. 1.53.5. The *bardocucullus* was a hooded cloak covering the whole body, worn principally by common people, and bearing some resemblance to the *paenula*, as to which cf. 14.130. Hence the juxtaposition here of the two names (K).

[f] Alluding, it is supposed, to a recent show.

129 Canusinae rufae

Roma magis fuscis vestitur, Gallia rufis,
　　et placet hic pueris militibusque color.

130 Paenula scortea

Ingrediare viam caelo licet usque sereno,
　　ad subitas nusquam scortea desit aquas.

131 Lacernae coccineae

Si veneto prasinove faves, qui coccina sumis,
　　ne fias ista transfuga sorte vide.

132 Pilleum

Si possem, totas cuperem misisse lacernas:
　　nunc tantum capiti munera mitto tuo.

133 Lacernae Baeticae

Non est lana mihi mendax nec mutor aheno.
　　sic placeant Tyriae: me mea tinxit ovis.

134 Fascia pectoralis

Fascia, crescentes dominae compesce papillas,
　　ut sit quod capiat nostra tegatque manus.

130.2 nusquam T : num- β : *vel hoc vel illud* γ
131.1 qui ... sumis γ : quid ... sumes Tβ

---

[a] The *paenula* was a closed garment, fitting closely,
with an opening for the head and a hood. It was an outer
garment, worn over the tunic in wet or cold weather, and
was made of frieze or leather (K).　　[b] Cf. 14.1.5.

BOOK XIV

129. Red Canusian cloak

Rome wears more browns, Gaul reds; and boys and soldiers like this color.

130. Leather overcoat

Though you start your journey with ever so clear a sky, never be without a leather coat[a] against sudden showers.

131. Scarlet coat

If you, who put on scarlet, support the blue or the green, mind this lot[b] doesn't make a deserter of you.

132. Cap

If I could, I should have wished to send you a whole cloak. As it is, I send a present for your head only.

133. Baetic cloak[c]

My wool does not lie and I am not changed by the vat. Let Tyrians find favor that way. As for me, my sheep dyed me.[d]

134. Breastband

Band, compress my lady's swelling breasts, so that my hand may find something to clasp and cover.

---

[c] The *lacerna* was a mantle fastened with a buckle, and not closed in like the *paenula*. It often had a hood and was ample, so that it could be worn over the toga (cf. Juv. 9.29) or other garment (K).   [d] Cf. 12.63.4.

135 (137)   Lacernae albae

Amphitheatrali nos commendamus ab usu,
  cum teget algentes alba lacerna togas.

136 (135)   Cenatoria

Nec fora sunt nobis nec sunt vadimonia nota:
  hoc opus est, pictis accubuisse toris.

137 (142)   Focale

Si recitaturus dedero tibi forte libellum,
  hoc focale tuas asserat auriculas.

138 (136)   Laena

Tempore brumali non multum levia prosunt:
  calfaciunt villi pallia vestra mei.

139 (138)   Mantele

Nobilius villosa tegant tibi lintea citrum:
  orbibus in nostris circulus esse potest.

135 (137). White cloaks

We recommend ourselves by our use in the
Amphitheater, when a white cloak[a] shall cover a
chilly gown.

136 (135). Dinner suits

Neither courts nor bail bonds are known to us. This
is our business, to recline on painted couches.

137 (142). Comforter

If perchance I am going to recite and send you an
invitation, let this comforter set your ears at
liberty.[b]

138 (136). Overcoat

In winter time smooth cloth is not much use. My
shag makes your mantles warm.

139 (138). Tablecloth

Let fleecy linen cloths cover your citrus more nobly.
On *my* found tables a circle[c] is acceptable.

[a] It was customary to wear white at public spectacles;
cf. 4.2.

[b] From boredom; cf. 4.41.2. *Asserere in libertatem*
("claim as free") was formulaic in the procedure for freeing
a slave; cf. 1.52.5.

[c] Made by wet round-footed vessels. M.'s tables were
ordinary ones.

140 (139) Cuculli Liburnici

Iungere nescisti nobis, o stulte, lacernas:
    indueras albas, exue callainas.

141 (140) Udones Cilicii

Non hos lana dedit sed olentis barba mariti:
    Cinyphio poterit planta latere sinu.

142 (141) Synthesis

Dum toga per quinas gaudet requiescere luces,
    hos poteris cultus sumere iure tuo.

143 Tunicae Patavinae

Vellera consumunt Patavinae multa trilices,
    et pingues tunicas serra secare potest.

---

[a] *Callainas* = the color of the *callais*, a stone which, according to Pliny (*N.H.* 37.151) *sapphirum imitatur, candidior et litoroso mari similis*, i.e. a kind of sea-green. The hood and mantle should have been of the same hue, as the green hood, wetted by rain, would be apt to stain the white mantle. Properly *callais* was blue turquoise, *callaica* green (K).

[b] *Cilicium* was a cloth made of goats' hair and garments or other articles made of it were called *cilicia*, even where, as here, the hair came from Africa, Cinyps being the name of a river near the Syrtes: cf. 7.95.13 (K).

[c] The *synthesis* was worn at the *Saturnalia*: cf. 14.1.1. It was ordinarily a dinner dress: cf. 5.79.2.

280

BOOK XIV

140 (139). Liburnian hoods

Foolish fellow, you did not know how to match your cloak with us. It was white when you put it on; take it off, and it's green.[a]

141 (140). Cilician socks

Wool did not supply these, but the beard of a smelly husband. The foot will be able to hide in a Cinyphian shelter.[b]

142 (141). Dinner suit

While the gown rejoices in a five-day rest, you can put these garments on with a clear conscience.[c]

143. Patavian tunics

Patavian triple-twill[d] uses up many a fleece, and a saw[e] can cut the thick tunics.

[d] The *trilix* was where every weft thread was passed over one and then under three of the warp threads, instead of over one and under the next in regular succession, as in ordinary weaving. The process is called twilling, and the fabric would be triple-twilled. Virgil speaks of a breastplate *auro trilix*: *Aen.* 3.467; i.e. chain mail (K).

[e] Usually taken as "only a saw," a linguistically legitimate rendering. But for less stiff material cutting with a saw would be inconvenient, if not impracticable.

144 Spongea

Haec tibi sorte datur tergendis spongea mensis
utilis, expresso cum levis imbre tumet.

145 Paenula gausapina

Is mihi candor inest, villorum gratia tanta est,
ut me vel media sumere messe velis.

146 Cervical

Tingue caput Cosmi folio, cervical olebit:
perdidit unguentum cum coma, pluma tenet.

147 Cubicularia gausapina

Stragula purpureis lucent villosa tapetis.
quid prodest si te congelat uxor anus?

148 Lodices

Nudo stragula ne toro paterent,
iunctae nos tibi venimus sorores.

145.1 tanta est $\beta\gamma$: t- T   148.2 uenimus $\beta\gamma$: caremus
T : cavimus *Heinsius*

---

[a] Frieze garments were ordinarily worn in winter: cf. 6.59.

[b] *Gausapum* was woollen cloth having, like frieze, a thick nap on one side only, as distinguished from *amphimallum*, which had a nap on both. It was introduced into Rome in the time of the Elder Pliny's father: Pliny *N.H.* 8.193 (K).

144. Sponge

This sponge is given you by lot; it is useful for wiping tables when it becomes light and swells after the water is squeezed out.

145. Frieze coat (paenula)

Such is my whiteness, such the beauty of my shag, that you would wish to put me on even in mid harvest.[a]

146. Pillow

Moisten your head with Cosmus' leaf, the pillow will smell; when your hair has lost the pomade, the feathers retain it.

147. Frieze blankets (cubicularia)

Your shaggy[b] blankets are bright with purple brocade. What is the good, if your aged wife freezes you up?

148. Small bedspreads (lodices)

Lest the blankets[c] on your bare bed show, we have come to you, sisters joined in one.

[c] The *lodix* was a small shaggy blanket. Sometimes two were sewed together to form a coverlet. The Emperor Augustus used it as a wrap for warmth in the open air: Suet. *Aug.* 83. *Lodices* came from Verona: cf. 14.152 (K).

149 Amictorium

Mammosas metuo; tenerae me trade puellae,
ut possint niveo pectore lina frui.

150 Cubicularia polymita

Haec tibi Memphitis tellus dat munera: victa est
pectine Niliaco iam Babylonos acus.

151 Zona

Longa satis nunc sum; dulci sed pondere venter
si tumeat, fiam tunc tibi zona brevis.

152 Gausapum quadratum

Lodices mittet docti tibi terra Catulli;
nos Helicaonia de regione sumus.

153 Semicinctium

Det tunicam locuples: ego te praecingere possum.
essem si locuples, munus utrumque darem.

---

[a] Damask is a variety of twill (cf. 14.143), and depends
upon the number of warp threads (generally four) inter-
sected by the weft (K).

[b] Babylon was celebrated for embroidery in color; the
art of many-threaded work (*polymita*) came from Alexan-
dria: cf. Pliny *N.H.* 8.196 (K).

BOOK XIV

149. Wrap

I fear big-breasted women. Hand me over to a young girl, so that my linen may enjoy a snowy bosom.

150. Damask blankets (cubicularia)[a]

The land of Memphis gives you this present; Babylon's needle[b] is surpassed now by the comb[c] of the Nile.

151. Girdle

I am long enough at present; but if your stomach should swell with a sweet burden, I should then be too short a girdle for you.

152. A square frieze rug

The country of poet Catullus will send you blankets (*lodices*); we are from the region of Helicaon.[d]

153. Apron

Let a rich man give you a tunic; I can gird you in front. If I were rich, I should give you both presents.

[c] A weaver's reed [or sley] (K).
[d] Paduan: cf. 10.93.1.

154 Lanae amethystinae

Ebria Sidoniae cum sim de sanguine conchae,
non video quare sobria lana vocer.

155 Lanae albae

Velleribus primis Apulia, Parma secundis
nobilis: Altinum tertia laudat ovis.

156 Lanae Tyriae

Nos Lacedaemoniae pastor donavit amicae:
deterior Ledae purpura matris erat.

157 Lanae Pollentinae

Non tantum pullo lugentes vellere lanas,
sed solet et calices haec dare terra suos.

158 Idem

Lana quidem tristis sed tonsis nata ministris,
quales non primo de grege mensa citat.

158.1 nata *Scriberius* : neta *Bongarsii marg.* : neca T : apta
$\beta\gamma$ 2 citat Tβ : uetat γ : vocat *ed. Rom.*

---

[a] "Amethyst" etymologically means "unintoxicated,"
either, as Pliny says (*N.H.* 37.121), because it did not
approximate to the color of wine, or because its possession
was supposed to be an antidote against inebriety. There
are similar Greek epigrams in *Pal. Anth.* 9.748 and 752
(K).

[b] Paris gave to Helen.

154. Amethystine wool

Since I am drunk with the blood of a Sidonian shellfish, I do not see why I am called sober wool.[a]

155. White wool

Apulia is famed for the best fleeces, Parma for the second best. The third best sheep gives praise to Altinum.

156. Tyrian wool

The shepherd gave us to his Lacedaemonian mistress.[b] Her mother Leda's purple was inferior.[c]

157. Wool from Pollentia[d]

This land is wont to supply not only wool that mourns with somber fleece but her cups also.

158. Same

The wool is sad to be sure, but suitable for cropped pages, such as the table does not summon from the pick of the corps.[e]

[c] Laconian purple was the finest produced in Europe, that of Tyre the finest in Asia: Pliny *N.H.* 9.127. The latter was superior to the former (K).

[d] Famed for its wool, which was black: Pliny *N.H.* 8.191.

[e] These inferior slaves would appear on humdrum occasions, by contrast with the long-haired boys of 2.57.5 and elsewhere.

159 Tomentum Leuconicum

Oppressae nimium vicina est fascia plumae?
vellera Leuconicis accipe rasa sagis.

160 Tomentum Circense

Tomentum concisa palus Circense vocatur.
haec pro Leuconico stramina pauper emit.

161 Pluma

Lassus Amyclaea poteris requiescere pluma,
interior cycni quam tibi lana dedit.

162 Faenum

Fraudata tumeat fragilis tibi culcita mula.
non venit ad duros pallida cura toros.

163 Tintinabulum

Redde pilam: sonat aes thermarum. ludere pergis?
Virgine vis sola lotus abire domum.

---

[a] Cf. 5.62.6.

[b] Thought to be so called because it was used in the circus on seats for the common people: cf. Sen. *Dial.* 7.25.2.

[c] I.e. Spartan (cf. 8.28.13). Swans were plentiful on the river Eurotas.

[d] Cf. Hor. *Od.* 3.1.21.

159. Leuconian stuffing

Is the bed girth[a] too close to the feather mattress you press down? Accept fleeces shorn for Leuconian cloaks.

160. Circensian stuffing

Marsh reed chopped up is called Circensian[b] stuffing. The poor man buys this straw instead of Leuconian.

161. Feathers

Tired you may rest on feathers of Amyclae[c] which the swan's inner down has given you.

162. Hay

Let your crackling mattress swell, cheating your mule. Pale care comes not to hard pallets.[d]

163. Bell

Return the ball.[e] The bell of the baths sounds. Do you go on playing? You want to go home with nothing but a wash in the Virgin.[f]

[e] Cf. on 46 above.

[f] The hot baths will be full, or closed, and he will have to content himself with a cold bath from the *aqua Virgo*; cf. 5.20.9.

MARTIAL

164 Discus

Splendida cum volitant Spartani pondera disci,
  este procul, pueri: sit semel ille nocens.

165 Cithara

Reddidit Eurydicen vati: sed perdidit ipse,
  dum sibi non credit nec patienter amat.

166 Idem

De Pompeiano saepe est eiecta theatro
  quae duxit silvas detinuitque feras.

167 Plectrum

Fervida ne trito tibi pollice pusula surgat,
  exornent docilem candida plectra lyram.

168 Trochus

Inducenda rota est: das nobis utile munus:
  iste trochus pueris, at mihi cantus erit.

---

[a] Apollo accidentally killed the Spartan boy Hyacinthus
with a quoit; cf. ep. 173. But *discus* also means "gong,"
hence its placing after the bell.

164. Quoit (gong)

When the shining weight of the Spartan quoit is flying, keep your distance, boys. Let it be guilty only once.[a]

165. Lyre

It gave Eurydice back to the bard; but he lost her himself, not trusting himself nor loving in moderation.[b]

166. Same

It has often been thrown out of Pompey's theater[c]— the instrument that drew forests and held wild beasts.[d]

167. Quill

Lest a hot blister arise on your chafed thumb, let a white quill[e] equip the docile lyre.

168. Hoop

The wheel must be fitted with a tire. You give me a useful present. This will be a hoop to boys, but a tire to me.

[b] Orpheus loved "not wisely, but too well"—the same sense as in 5.7.8.

[c] I.e. hissed off by the audience.

[d] When played by Orpheus.

[e] An instrument for striking the strings.

169 Idem

Garrulus in laxo cur anulus orbe vagatur?
  cedat ut argutis obvia turba trochis.

170 Signum Victoriae aureum

Haec illi sine sorte datur cui nomina Rhenus
  vera dedit. deciens adde Falerna, puer.

171 Βρούτου παιδίον fictile

Gloria tam parvi non est obscura sigilli:
  istius pueri Brutus amator erat.

172 Sauroctonos Corinthius

Ad te reptanti, puer insidiose, lacertae
  parce; cupit digitis illa perire tuis.

ᵃ Rings were often strung round the orbit of a boy's hoop: see a picture taken from a sepulchral bas-relief at Tivoli reproduced in Rich's *Dict. Ant. s.v.* "Anulus." How the hoop was able to run is very obscure (K).

169. Same

Why do noisy rings[a] wander round the wide circle?
So that the crowd in their path may yield to the tin-
kling hoops.

170. Gold statue of Victory[b]

She is given without drawing of lot to him to whom
Rhine has given a true name. Ten times pour the
Falernian, boy.[c]

171. "Brutus' Boy" in clay

Not dim is the glory of so small a figurine.[d] This is
the boy Brutus loved.

172. Lizard slayer in Corinthian bronze[e]

Spare the lizard, insidious boy, as she creeps toward
you; she wants to die by your fingers.

[b] This, and the following, describe *sigilla* (statuettes)
which were frequently given at the Saturnalia, i.e. on the
last two days, which were called *sigillaria*: cf. Auson. *De
Fer. Rom* 32 (*festa sigillorum nomine dicta colunt*) (K).

[c] To represent the letters of Germanicus (Domitian): cf.
9.93.

[d] Cf. 2.77.4; 9.50.5. There may be a play on two senses
of *amator*, which can also mean "fan" (cf. "amateur"). Cf.
Pliny *N.H.* 34.82 *puerum, quem amando Brutus Philip-
piensis cognomine suo illustravit.*

[e] On a replica of a work of Praxiteles representing the
young Apollo with an arrow watching a lizard. It was
called Σαυρόκτονος ("Lizard-killer"): Pliny *N.H.* 34.70.

173 Hyacinthus in tabula pictus

Flectit ab inviso morientia lumina disco
  Oebalius, Phoebi culpa dolorque, puer.

174 Hermaphroditus marmoreus

Masculus intravit fontis: emersit utrumque:
  pars est una patris, cetera matris habet.

175 Danae picta

Cur a te pretium Danae, regnator Olympi,
  accepit, gratis si tibi Leda dedit?

176 Persona Germana

Sum figuli lusus russi persona Batavi.
  quae tu derides, haec timet ora puer.

BOOK XIV

173. Painting of Hyacinthus[a]

The Oebalian boy, Phoebus' fault and sorrow, turns
dying eyes from the hateful quoit.

174. Hermaphroditus in marble

He entered the fountain a male; he came out
double-sexed. One part is his father's; the rest he
has of his mother.

175. Painting of Danae[b]

Why, ruler of Olympus, did Danae receive a price
from you, if Leda gave herself to you for nothing?

176. German mask

I am a jest of the potter, mask of a red-haired Bata-
vian. The face you mock, a boy fears.[c]

---

[a] See 14.164n. The picture alluded to may be a copy of
the one by Nicias of Athens (fourth century B.C.), the origi-
nal of which was transported to Rome by Augustus on the
capture of Alexandria: Pliny *N.H.* 35.131.

[b] Possibly a copy of Artemon's picture of Danae *miran-
tibus eam praedonibus*: cf. Pliny *N.H.* 35.139 (K).

[c] To him it is a bogey.

177 Hercules Corinthius

Elidit geminos infans nec respicit anguis.
 iam poterat teneras Hydra timere manus.

178 Hercules fictilis

Sum fragilis: sed tu, moneo, ne sperne sigillum:
 non pudet Alciden nomen habere meum.

179 Minerva argentea

Dic mihi, virgo ferox, cum sit tibi cassis et hasta,
 quare non habeas aegida. 'Caesar habet.'

180 Europe picta

Mutari melius tauro, pater optime divum,
 tunc poteras Io cum tibi vacca fuit.

177. Hercules in Corinthian bronze

The infant strangles two snakes without looking at them. Already the Hydra might fear his tender hands.

178. Hercules in clay[a]

I am fragile, but I warn you, do not scorn the figurine. Alcides is not ashamed to bear my name.[b]

179. Minerva in silver

Tell me, fierce virgin, since you have helm and spear, why you don't have the aegis. "Caesar has it."[c]

180. Painting of Europa

You could better have been changed to a bull, most excellent Father of the Gods, when Io was your cow.

---

[a] Pliny (*N.H.* 35 157) mentions such a statue done by one Vulca of Veii in the time of Tarquinius Priscus.

[b] An odd way of saying "Alcides is not ashamed to have me bear his name." Perhaps a deliberate touch of humor—the little statue feels that he is the real Alcides.

[c] See the description of Domitian's breastplate, 7.1, 2.

181   Leandros marmoreus

Clamabat tumidis audax Leandros in undis:
'mergite me, fluctus, cum rediturus ero.'

182   Sigillum gibberi fictile

Ebrius haec fecit terris, puto, monstra Prometheus:
Saturnalicio lusit et ipse luto.

183   Homeri Batrachomyomachia

Perlege Maeonio cantatas carmine ranas
et frontem nugis solvere disce meis.

184   Homerus in pugillaribus membraneis

Ilias et Priami regnis inimicus Ulixes
multiplici pariter condita pelle latent.

185   Vergili Culex

Accipe facundi Culicem, studiose, Maronis,
ne nucibus positis 'arma virumque' legas.

183 lemm. batrachomachia *vel sim.* αβγ : *corr. Calderinus*

---

[a] Real hunchbacks, made originally (like the statuettes given as presents at the Saturnalia) from clay, by Prometheus (cf. 10.39.4).

[b] "If Homer can unbend, I can be excused."

BOOK XIV

181. Leander in marble

Bold Leander cried amid the swelling waves:
"Drown me, ye billows, when I am on my way back."

182. Clay figurine of a hunchback

Methinks Prometheus was drunk when he made
these monsters[a] for the earth. He too jested with
Saturnalian clay.

183. Homer's "Battle of Frogs and Mice"

Read through the frogs sung in Maeonian song and
learn to relax your brow with my trifles.[b]

184. Homer in parchment notebooks

The *Iliad* and Ulysses, foe to Priam's realm, lie
together, stored in many layers of skin.[c]

185. Virgil's "Gnat"

Accept, studious reader, the "Gnat"[d] of eloquent
Maro; no need to read "Arms and the Man," when
you put away your nuts.[e]

[c] I.e. in a codex; see W. V. Harris in *Renaissance Society
and Culture* (New York, 1991), 78f. Read *Ilios*, 'Troy'?
[d] Cf. 8.55.20n.
[e] For gambling. When the Saturnalia was over and
reading recommenced, something lighter than the *Aeneid*
would be to hand.

186 Vergilius in membranis

Quam brevis immensum cepit membrana Maronem!
ipsius vultus prima tabella gerit.

187 Μενάνδρου Θαΐς

Hac primum iuvenum lascivos lusit amores;
nec Glycera pueri, Thais amica fuit.

188 Cicero in membranis

Si comes ista tibi fuerit membrana, putato
carpere te longas cum Cicerone vias.

189 Monobyblos Properti

Cynthia, facundi carmen iuvenale Properti,
accepit famam, nec minus ipsa dedit.

190 Titus Livius in membranis

Pellibus exiguis artatur Livius ingens,
quem mea non totum bibliotheca capit.

---

[a] Cf. 1.53.2n.

[b] As interpreted in my edition, "Thais" was Menander's
first love-comedy; and the mistress of the youth in the play
was called Thais, not Glycera, which was the name of
Menander's own mistress.

[c] The first Book of Propertius' elegies was entitled "Cyn-
thia," but the title "Monobiblos," seemingly deriving from
M.'s heading, is found in some of his manuscripts. If it

186. Virgil on parchment

How small a quantity of parchment has comprised vast Maro! The first leaf bears his own countenance.[a]

187. Menander's "Thais"

With her he first played with young men's wanton love; but the boy's mistress was not Glycera but Thais.[b]

188. Cicero on parchment

If this parchment will be your companion, suppose yourself to be making a long journey with Cicero.

189. The "Monobiblos" of Propertius[c]

Cynthia, the youthful song of eloquent Propertius, received fame, and herself bestowed it no less.

190. Titus Livius on parchment

Vast Livy,[d] for whom complete my library does not have room, is compressed in tiny skins.

refers to Book I, it will have originated after later publications, since, as G. P. Goold says in his Loeb edition (p. 17), "a priori it is unlikely that a young poet should so describe his first book." In Goold's view it "ought to mean 'Propertius in a single volume' (i.e. a collection of the poet's work, and most obviously an anthology)." But 'youthful' points to Book I.

[d] In 142 books.

191 Sallustius

Hic erit, ut perhibent doctorum corda virorum,
    primus Romana Crispus in historia.

192 Ovidi Metamorphosis in membranis

Haec tibi multiplici quae structa est massa tabella,
    carmina Nasonis quinque decemque gerit.

193 Tibullus

Ussit amatorem Nemesis lasciva Tibullum,
    in tota iuvit quem nihil esse domo.

194 Lucanus

Sunt quidam qui me dicant non esse poetam:
    sed qui me vendit bybliopola putat.

195 Catullus

Tantum magna suo debet Verona Catullo,
    quantum parva suo Mantua Vergilio.

196 Calvi de aquae frigidae usu

Haec tibi quae fontes et aquarum nomina dicit,
    ipsa suas melius charta natabat aquas.

---

[a] I.e. books.

[b] It was "Delia" of whom Tibullus (1.5.30) writes *at iuvet in tota me nihil esse domo*; "Nemesis" was his second love.

[c] Presumed to be C. Licinius Calvus, Catullus' friend

BOOK XIV

191. Sallust

Here will be Crispus, foremost of Roman historians,
so the judgment of learned men declares.

192. Ovid's "Metamorphoses" in parchment

This mass that has been built up for you with many
a leaf contains the fifteen lays[a] of Naso.

193. Tibullus

Wanton Nemesis inflamed her lover Tibullus, who
"was happy to be a cipher in all his house."[b]

194. Lucan

There are some who say I am no poet; but the book-
seller who vends me thinks I am.

195. Catullus

Great Verona owes as much to her Catullus as does
little Mantua to her Virgil.

196. Calvus[c] on the use of cold water

These pages that tell you of fountains and the
names of rivers were better swimming in their own
waters.[d]

and fellow poet, with whom he is regularly associated. The
work in question is unknown, and M.'s uncomplimentary
judgment surprises. If this were a different Calvus, the
juxtaposition with Catullus could be a joke on M.'s part.

[d] From which the papyrus came.

197 Mulae pumilae

His tibi de mulis non est metuenda ruina:
altius in terra paene sedere soles.

198 Catella Gallicana

Delicias parvae si vis audire catellae,
narranti brevis est pagina tota mihi.

199 Asturco

Hic brevis ad numeros rapidum qui colligit unguem,
venit ab auriferis gentibus Astur equus.

200 Canis vertragus

Non sibi sed domino venatur vertragus acer,
illaesum leporem qui tibi dente feret.

201 Palaestrita

Non amo quod vincit, sed quod succumbere novit
et didicit melius τὴν ἐπικλινοπάλην.

197.2 paene βγ : saepe T   199.1 numeros T : -rum
βγ   201.1 uincit βγ : -cat T

---

[a] Cf. M.'s description of Issa (1.109).
[b] This small horse had a special sort of trot (Pliny *N.H.*
8.166).

197. Dwarf mules

You need not be afraid of falling off these mules.
You are almost higher up sitting on the ground.

198. Gallic lapdog

If you want to hear of the pretty tricks of the little
lapdog, a whole page is too short for me in the
telling.[a]

199. Jennet

This little Asturian horse[b] that picks up its fleet
hooves in rhythm came from gold-bearing peoples.

200. Greyhound[c]

The keen greyhound hunts not for himself but for
his master; he will bring you a hare unharmed by
his tooth.

201. Wrestler

I like him, not because he wins, but because he
knows how to lie low and has better learned "lean-
to" wrestling.[d]

[c] *Vertragus*, a Celtic word, probably meaning "fast
runner."

[d] *Succumbere*, lit. "lie underneath," can also mean
"yield." There is a pun on κλίνη (klinê) = "bed." Domitian
called sexual intercourse *clinopale*, "bed wrestling" (Suet.
Dom. 22).

202 Simius

Callidus emissas eludere simius hastas,
si mihi cauda foret, cercopithecus eram.

203 Puella Gaditana

Tam tremulum crisat, tam blandum prurit, ut ipsum
masturbatorem fecerit Hippolytum.

204 Cymbala

Aera Celaenaeos lugentia Matris amores
esuriens Gallus vendere saepe solet.

205 Puer

Sit nobis aetate puer, non pumice levis,
propter quem placeat nulla puella mihi.

206 Cestos

Collo necte, puer, meros amores,
ceston de Veneris sinu calentem.

202. Monkey

A monkey, cunning at avoiding darts flung at me, I should be a long-tailed ape[a] if I had a tail.

203. Girl from Gades

Her waggles are so tremulous, her itch so seductive that she would make a masturbator out of Hippolytus[b] himself.

204. Cymbals

The hungry eunuch-priest is often wont to sell bronzes that mourn the Celaenaean darling[c] of the Mother.

205. Boy

Let me have a boy made smooth by youth, not pumice stone, on whose account no girl will please me.

206. Cestus

Bind round your neck, boy, a cestus[d] warm from Venus' bosom, love undiluted.

[a] The *cercopithecus* came from Aethiopia: Pliny *N.H.* 8.72. In Egypt it was a sacred animal: Juv. 15.4.
[b] Type of chastity.
[c] Attis.
[d] Cf. 6.13.5.

207 Idem

Sume Cytheriaco medicatum nectare ceston:
    ussit amatorem balteus iste Iovem.

208 Notarius

Currant verba licet, manus est velocior illis:
    nondum lingua suum, dextra peregit opus.

209 Concha

Levis ab aequorea cortex Mareotica concha
    fiat: inoffensa curret harundo via.

210 Morio

Non mendax stupor est nec fingitur arte dolosa.
    quisquis plus iusto non sapit, ille sapit.

211 Caput vervecinum

Mollia Phrixei secuisti colla mariti.
    hoc meruit tunicam qui tibi, saeve, dedit?

---

[a] Hera borrowed from Aphrodite her *cestus* to inflame
the ardor of Zeus: Hom. *Il.* 14.214–221.

207. Same

Take a cestus, treated with Cytherean nectar. This girdle burned amorous Jupiter.[a]

208. Stenographer

Though the words speed, the hand is faster than they. The right hand has finished its work, while the tongue has more to do.[b]

209. Seashell

Let the Mareotic bark[c] be smoothed with the seashell; the reed will run its course without hindrance.

210. Idiot

His stupidity does not lie, is not feigned by wily art. He that is witless to excess has his wits.

211. Ram's head

You cut the soft throat of the Phrixian[d] husband of the flock. Did he deserve this, who gave you, cruel man, your tunic?

[b] Not only does the stenographer keep pace with the speaker, he runs ahead anticipating words to come.

[c] Papyrus. Pliny (*N.H.* 13.81) says that papyrus was smoothed by an ivory instrument or by a shell, but that the writing fades.

[d] Called "Phrixian" from the legendary ram with the golden fleece that carried Phrixus across the Hellespont.

MARTIAL

212 Pumilus

Si solum spectes hominis caput, Hectora credas:
si stantem videas, Astyanacta putes.

213 Parma

Haec, quae saepe solet vinci, quae vincere raro,
parma tibi, scutum pumilionis erit.

214 Comoedi pueri

Non erit in turba quisquam Μισούμενος ista:
sed poterit quivis esse Δὶς ἐξαπατῶν.

215 Fibula

Dic mihi simpliciter, comoedis et citharoedis,
fibula, quid praestas? 'carius ut futuant.'

216 (218) Auceps

Non tantum calamis sed cantu fallitur ales,
callida dum tacita crescit harundo manu.

212. Dwarf

If you looked only at the man's head, you would believe him Hector; if you saw him standing, you would think him Astyanax.

213. Buckler

Wont often to be defeated and to be victorious rarely,[a] this will be to you a buckler, but the shield of a dwarf.

214. Boy comic actors

No one will be "The Hated One" in this company; but any one of them can be "The Double Deceiver."[b]

215. Fibula

Tell me candidly, fibula, what is it you do for comic actors and singers?[c] "Get them a higher price for their fucking."

216 (218). Fowler

The bird is deceived not only by rods but by song, as the cunning reed lengthens in the silent hand.

[a] Cf. 9.68.8n.
[b] Two lost comedies of Menander.
[c] Cf. 7.82.2; 11.75.3.

MARTIAL

217 (216) Accipiter

Praedo fuit volucrum: famulus nunc aucupis idem
decipit et captas non sibi maeret aves.

218 (217) Opsonator

Dic quotus et quanti cupias cenare nec unum
addideris verbum: cena parata tibi est.

219 Cor bubulum

Pauper causidicus nullos referentia nummos
carmina cum scribas, accipe cor quod habes.

220 Cocus

Non satis est ars sola coco: servire palatum
nolo: cocus domini debet habere gulam.

221 Craticula cum veribus

Rara tibi curva craticula sudet ofella;
spumeus in longa cuspide fumet aper.

BOOK XIV

217 (216). Hawk

He was a pirate to birds; now as the fowler's servant
he seizes them and grieves that they are not caught
for himself.[a]

218 (217). Caterer

Say how many you want to dine and for how much,
and don't add another word; your dinner is ready.

219. Bullock's heart

Since, a pauper barrister, you write poems that
bring in no money, accept the heart[b] you have.

220. Cook

Art alone is not enough for a cook. I would not have
his palate in slavery. A cook should have the taste
of his master.

221. Gridiron with spits

Let your grated gridiron sweat with the round mor-
sel; let the foaming boar steam on a long spit.

[a] See my edition.
[b] *Cor*, with a play on the secondary sense ("intelli-
gence"), as in 6.64.18.

222 Pistor dulciarius

Mille tibi dulces operum manus ista figuras
extruet: huic uni parca laborat apis.

223 Adipata

Surgite: iam vendit pueris ientacula pistor
cristataeque sonant undique lucis aves.

222. Confectioner

This hand will construct for you a thousand sweet shapes of handicraft; the thrifty bee works only for him.

223. Children's Dainties[a]

Rise. Already the baker is selling boys their breakfast, and the crested birds of daybreak sound from every side.

[a] *Adipata* are for children also in Juv. 6.631.

APPENDIX A

ADDITIONAL NOTES

5.37   Puella senibus voce dulcior cycnis,
                agna Galaesi mollior Phalantini.

The reasons for the emendation *voce dulcior* (*dulcior mihi*
codd.) in v. 1 are briefly given in the critical note to my
Teubner edition, but some amplification may be called for.
Here we have a classic specimen of interpolative corrup-
tion, in that the text contains a word not only unwanted
but actually inappropriate and lacks a word that is essen-
tial.

Mihi is inept. The comparison between the little girl
and aged swans, like the following series, must not be
given as the poet's personal opinion. When Burns tells us
that his love is like the red, red rose or Byron that she
walks in beauty like the night, they do not add "to my eyes"
or the like. Erotion *was* sweet-voiced, soft, delicate, and
the rest, as vv. 4ff unequivocally declare. The length of the
interval precludes taking *mihi* as ethic dative with *tepet
busto* in 14, not that anyone is likely to do that.

On the other side of the coin, the epithet *dulcis* relates
primarily to taste. It can be transferred to sound or smell,
but then a limiting word is needed. Honey is sweet; aged
swans are sweet only in respect of their voices: Sen.
Phaedr. 302 *dulcior vocem moriente cycno*; Stat. *Theb.*
5.341 *mitior et senibus cycnis . . . vox.* The trouble probably

317

started with one of those inversions common in the manuscripts, *dulcior voce*. Since *voce* would not scan in its new position, it was replaced by the first iambic word that came to hand.

7.34.8   'quid? tu tot domini deique nostri
                praefers muneribus Neronianas
                thermas?' praefero balneis cinaedi.

So in my Teubner text (see *SB*[1]). I have since noticed that M., unlike Catullus, avoids a break after the first foot of a hendecasyllable except when there is also a break before it, as in 2.83.5 *erras: iste potest et irrumare.* Although an isolated case is not inconceivable, it will be safer thus:

                'quid? tu tot domini deique nostri
                praefers muneribus Neronianas?'
                thermas praefero balneis cinaedi.

Thermas understood with *Neronianas* is no problem, especially after *thermas* in v. 5; cf. *Marcellano* (sc. *theatro*) in 2.29.5 and *Marcelli Pompeianumque* in 10.51.11. There is a contrast between the *thermae* of Nero, one of the three great public baths, and the privately built *balnea*.

10.81   Cum duo venissent ad Phyllida mane fututum
                et nudam cuperet sumere uterque prior,
             promisit pariter se Phyllis utrique daturam,
                et dedit: ille pedem sustulit, hic tunicam.

In *Classical Philology* 73 (1978). 288 I raised two objections to the usual interpretation: (a) Why did Lover No 2 raise the tunic? If it be answered *ut paedicaret* (cf. Schrevel, ἅμα πρόσσω καὶ ὀπίσσω λεύσσουσα), it has to be asked why this should have been any less needful in the case of No 1. (b) On the assumption that Phyllis' promise was meant seriously, this would be no way to keep it. No 2 did not come *paedicatum*.

318

Two more objections may be added. In the position implied by *pedem sustulit* the tunic would have to be drawn down, not up. (b) Phyllis was not wearing a tunic (2 *nudam*).

"Phyllis 'gave' to both, but to No 1 she gave herself, to No 2 her tunic." That involves a small liberty in that Phyllis is said to give the tunic, whereas in fact she merely did nothing to prevent the theft (at least it would appear so). That would hardly trouble Martial, intent on his word play.

11.14 Heredes, nolite brevem sepelire colonum:
    nam terra est illi quantulacumque gravis.

Commentators remind us that *sit tibi terra levis* was a common prayer for the dead, but that is not the end of the matter. A small man is no more oppressed by weight proportionate to his size than a big man. And how small does one have to be to find *any* weight, however slight, burdensome? But the epigram is not about just any small person, it is about a farmer. Farmers have a special concern with earth; they dig it, plow it, even carry it. An undersized farmer will find the work heavier than his burly peers. So any earth on top of him is *gravis*, "heavy / disagreeable."

11.95 Incideris quotiens in basia fellatorum,
    in solium puta te mergere, Flacco, caput.

Solium is interpreted as a bathtub in which *fellatores* have washed; there is nothing in the Latin to say so. Furthermore, even such a tub would be less, not more, disagreeable than actual kisses. *Solium*, from recollections of 2.42, 2.70, and 6.81, has replaced another word, whether *lasanum* (as John Bodel suggested to me) or, it may be, *trullam*. The sense of *trulla* here required is found in Juvenal, 3.108 *si trulla inverso crepitum dedit aurea fundo* (cf. Mart.

ADDITIONAL NOTES

1.37 *ventris onus misero, nec te pudet, excipis auro*), where commentators tend to doubt it for the frivolous reason that it occurs nowhere else. But it is guaranteed by *rectum minxit* in the previous line, it is a natural variation of the normal meaning, "ladle" (and cf. *trulleus*, "basin"), and only perversity refuses to recognize the same sense of τορύνη in Plut. *Vit. Anton.* 62.

12.52

As it stands, this epitaph defies interpretation. The lady to whom it is addressed had left her husband for a lover, who must be the deceased Rufus: for (a) *vestra* in v. 10, referring to the pair, cannot be divorced from *ille tuus Rufus* of v. 3 without dire confusion; (b) 1–4 should lead up to 5–6; (c) the ardent lover of v. 4 must surely be Paris' counterpart, the hero of the "rape" which is the theme of the poem; (d) nothing suggests that the husband was notorious (v. 3 *ille*). But vv. 7–8 tell us that the lady left her lover to go back to her husband, and that puts everything out of joint. Why celebrate an abortive escapade of which neither wife nor husband would have cause to be proud, and why should a "rape" with such an ending amaze Helen and absolve Paris? Moreover this couplet comes awkwardly between the previous and the following, which without it cohere perfectly. I regard it as an interpolation (cf. Sp. 26.7–8 and the spurious epigram 3.3) by a perhaps moralistically minded reader who mistook Rufus for the husband and thought that further explanation was called for.

12.62

Terentius Priscus, a patron of M.'s, presumed to be identical with the dedicatee of Plutarch's dialogue *On the cessa-*

tion of the oracles, is addressed in the introductory letter to
Book XII. He had returned from Rome to Bilbilis and
given a feast at the Saturnalia, as was his custom (v. 5).
The belief that it was given by his father to celebrate his
homecoming rests on a misunderstanding of v. 14, where
pater refers to Priscus himself. He is a father of children
(like Saturn himself, *pater optime* in v. 7), and of frugal
habit, which makes it the more remarkable that he should
put on so splendid a festivity.

Thus the distinction, originating with Immisch (see *RE*
Terentius 63), between Priscus senior and Priscus junior
in M.'s epigrams, is an illusion, arising from an incorrect
reading of this one.

13.15   Ligna acapna
            Si vicina tibi Nomento rura coluntur,
               ad villam moneo, rustice, ligna feras.
Nomento is clearly dative with *vicino*, not locative ablative
(cf. K.–S. I.477), and we have no warrant for taking *villam*
as M.'s villa. Why indeed should he expect laborers not his
own to bring him wood? And what of "smokeless"? Rather
it would appear that M. is offering some neighborly advice:
"Get your wood under cover, so that it will be dry and
smoke-free" (Walter). Ker calls the district of Nomentum
"marshy," whereas M. calls it dry (12.57.1). But dry as it
might be, at least in summer, there would be some rain.

13.118   Tarraco, Campano tantum cessura Lyaeo,
                  haec genuit *Tuscis* aemula vina cadis.
Tuscan wines get a bad rating in 1.26.6, where they are
coupled with Paelignian, which were only fit for freedmen
(13.121). Tarraco wines, on the other hand, are praised by
Pliny (*N.H.* 14.71) as famous for their elegance, compar-

321

able to the finest Italian. Friedländer was right to obelize *Tuscis*, except that he and the rest of us should have accepted Gilbert's *Latiis*, which seems authenticated by the echo in Sil. 3.369 *dat Tarraco pubem / vitifera et Latio tantum cessura Lyaeo*. In both *Latius* = "Italian." This echo has been previously unnoticed, it would seem. At any rate it is not mentioned in Gilbert's edition or Friedländer's. Since v. 617 of Silius' third Book refers to Domitian's Sarmatian war of 92, whereas the Xenia are assigned to 84 or 85 (see Friedländer, pp. 51f), Silius appears to be the borrower.

A combination of haplography and dittography may have produced *tiistis* = *tuscis*.

APPENDIX B

THE FICTITIOUS NAMES

Martial's epigrams are usually addressed to a named individual, real or imaginary, and other individuals are mentioned in the third person. Not seldom the addressee has no apparent connection with the subject in hand, e.g. Maximus in 1.69 or Flaccus in 1.98.

Many epigrams are offensive or defamatory. We have Martial's word for it in the prefatory letter to Book I and often elsewhere that in these he did not use real names nor aim at real people under pseudonyms; and in fact the insults are often too general to be recognized as applying to anybody in particular. The invented names may be Roman, whether praenomina like Quintus or Sextus or nomina or cognomina, or Greek. Boy slaves (often sex-objects), "loose women," and doctors generally have Greek names, though there are exceptions, like the boy Secundus in 12.75 or the doctor Fannius in 10.56. Some of the boys were real, like Voconius Victor's Thestylus in 7.29 and 8.63. Others may have been. Spendophorus of 9.56 has the appearance of actuality, but the name recurs in 10.83 in company with Telesphorus, who may be real there and in 11.26 but surely not in 11.58. It is quite possible that a real boy's name was applied to a figment, just as names of Martial's real friends and addressees are also used of imaginary figures in unflattering contexts; Rufus for example in 3.94 and 9.88. Paulus, evidently a real friend or acquaintance in 7.72, is a plagiarist in 2.20, a fake invalid in 9.85, and a bad judge of friends and antiques in 12.69. In all but one of Lupus' eleven appearances he is or may be fictive and his alleged activities show no consistent pattern; but in 10.48 he is in company with five friends of Martial whose reality is not in doubt. Publius (was he otherwise unscannable?) is real for the most part, but hardly in 10.98. As for doctors, of whom there are at least fourteen, none of them occur more than once except Alcon (twice) and Symmachus (three times). They could all be fictive.

Martial was not much in the habit of creating personalities, people who crop up repeatedly under the same name with similar characteristics. The outrageous and almost ubiquitous Zoilus, who is absent only in Books VII–X, is unique. Not only does he conform to his description in 11.92.2 ("not a vicious man, but Vice"), he is presented with enough variety to make him flesh and blood; whereas the plagiarist Fidentinus in Book I, the kisser Postumus and the dinner chaser Selius in Book II, and the poet-pest of three almost contiguous epigrams of Book III (44, 45, 50) are lay figures. Even these do not have counterparts in the later Books, though the Lesbian Philaenis in 7.67 reappears in 70, as does Labienus in 12.33 following 16. Carryovers from Book to Book, Zoilus excepted, are rare and insignificant. Philomelus is a rich man in 3.31 and 4.5, an old man in 3.93. Lycoris is dusky in 1.72 and goes to Tibur for remedy in 4.62, which looks like a first draft of 7.13. Diadumenus (3.65; 5.46; 6.34) is one of many catamites, Symmachus (5.9; 6.70; 7.18) one of many doctors, Chione one of many prostitutes, though her reality is pretended in 3.97. For the most part the commoner names serve their immediate purpose irrespective of their past or future. To track Lesbia or Galla through their numerous manifestations would be a waste of time.

Most of the imaginary names were doubtless chosen at random, but now and again they relate to their context. The link may be etymological: the lady's maid Plecusa, the castrated Glyptus, the hag Vetustilla, the eunuch Thelys, the dexterous barber Eutrapelus, the fiery Phlogis, the (sometimes) frigid Chione, the female doctor Hygia and the male Hyginus. Or association may determine the choice: we have a doctor Hippocrates, a luxurious Sardanapallus, a virtuous Lucretia, Thaises galore (cf. Lais in 3.11), a debauched Sotades, a catamite Ganymede. The greedy Parthenopaeus in 11.86 was not so called for nothing, and the reality of "fair Hylas" in 3.19 is at least dubious (cf. 11.28; but Hylas in 8.9 has no hint of his mythical homonym). In at least two cases the original of a name was a recent celebrity, one being the poisoner Pontia (2.34; 4.43; Juv. 6.638), who is addressed as alive and dangerous in 6.75. The other is the sodomitic Hamillus of 7.62, identifiable with the pederastic schoolmaster of Juv. 10.224. Verification comes from two Pompeian graffiti in which his name is significantly spelled backwards (see Friedländer, p. 545). It seems reasonable to assume that both were legally convicted (he perhaps under the Scantinian law, enforced by Domitian; Suet. *Dom.* 8.3) and so became notorious. Cerylus in 1.67 is likely to make a third example.

Horace's *Satires* often bring in to us obscure names as illustrating characteristics indicated by the context. Martial is not so much given to this, but note Priscus and Spanius in 2.41, Fuficulanus and Faventinus in 2.74, Julianus in 3.25, Silia or Pilia (by my conjecture) in

10.65.11, and Cydas' Hermeros in 10.83. Their reality may be doubted, and even if they were real, he cannot have expected his readers all over the world to recognize them, to say nothing of posterity.

INDEX OF TOPICS

327

INDEX OF TOPICS

331

IV.56. V.39. VI.62; 63. VIII.27.
IX.8; 48; 88. XI.44; 55; 67; 83.
XII.10. *cf.* I.10. II.26. III.52.
XII.40; 48; 90

    Moneylenders: II.44; 74
    Spendthrift: III.10. IV.66.
V.70. IX.82

OLD, UGLY
    Crones: I.19; 100. III.32; 76;
93. IV.20. VII.75. VIII.79.
IX.29; 37; 80. X.39; 67; 90.
XI.87. *cf.* VI.40. XII.23
    Old men: III.43; IV.36; 50;
53; 78. VII.9. XI.44; 46; 71; 81.
cf. VI.74. VIII.57
    Ugliness, deformity, etc.:
I.10. II.33; 35; 41; 87. III.8 (*cf.*
11); 39; 42; 72; 89; 98. IV.65.
V.43. VI.78. VII.38. VIII.59; 60.
X.99. XI.101. XII.22; 54; 83. *cf.*
III.51. IV.36. XI.21; 102. Bald:
III.74. V.49. VI.57; 74. X.83.
XII.7; 23; 45; 89. *cf.* VI.12.
XII.82.9

PRESENTS: I.111. II.39. IV.28;
56; 61. V.29; 39; 42; 59; 68.
VI.75. VII.16; 31; 36; 42; 46; 49;
55; 78. VIII.27; 28; 33. IX.48;
49; 72; 88. X.17; 57; 73; 94.
XI.18; 27; 29; 49; 89; 105.
XII.31; 36; 65. At Saturnalia:
II.85. IV.19; 46; 88. V.18; 19;
30; 84. VII.53 (list); 72; 91.
X.29. XII. 81; *cf.* VII.28. X.18;
88. XII.62. On Kinsfolk Day:
IX.54; 55. At Matronalia: V.84.
On recovery from illness
(*soteria*): XII.56. Thanks for:
X.73. See BIRTHDAY, MONEY
(gifts, legacy hunting)

PUFFS AND COMPLIMENTARY
ADDRESSES: I.7 (Stella); 8
(Decianus); 36 (Lucanus and
Tullus); 39 (Decianus); 70
(Proculus); 111 (Regulus). II.90
(Quintilian). III.6
(Marcellinus). IV.13 (Pudens
and Claudia Peregrina); 14
(Silius); 23 (Bruttianus); 75
(Nigrina). V.30 (Varro). VI.21
(Stella and Violentilla); 25
(Marcellinus). VII.44 and 45
(Ovidius); 47 (Licinius Sura);
56 (Rabirius); 63 (Silius); 69
(Theophila); 74 (Carpus and
Norbana). VIII.45 (Priscus and
Flaccus); 66 (Silius); 70
(Nerva); 73 (Istantius); 77
(Liber); 78 (Stella). IX.epist.
(Stertinius Avitus); 26 (Nerva);
72 (Liber); 84 (Norbanus); 99
(Antonius Primus). X.20
(Pliny); 23 and 32 (Antonius
Primus); 33 (Munatius Gallus);
35 and 38 (Calenus and
Sulpicia); 37 (Maternus); 78
(Macer); 87 (Restitutus). XI.48
and 50 (Silius); 53 (Claudia
Rufina). XII.3 (Priscus); 21
(Marcella). *cf.* I.54 (Fuscus); 55
(Fronto) 61 (Licinianus). IV.55
(Licinianus) XII.62 (Priscus)

RACING, CHARIOTEERS,
RACEHORSES: III.63,12. IV.67.
V.25. VI.46. VII.7. VIII.11. X.9;
48.23; 50; 53; 74; 76. XI.1; 33

RECITATION: I.29; 38; 52. II.20;
88. III.18. IV.41. VI.48. VIII.20;
76. IX.83. X.70.10. XII.63. *cf.*
I.63; 76.10. See DINNERS

INDEX OF TOPICS

INDEX OF TOPICS

335

INDEX OF TOPICS

INDEX OF NAMES

NOTE: Certainly or probably fictitious names are marked with an asterisk. Italics denote names that do not appear in the text.

INDEX OF NAMES

INDEX OF NAMES

Odyssey: IV.64.29. VII.42.
X.94. XII.31. *cf.* VIII.68.1

*Alcon, doctor: VI.70. XI.84.5

Alexander the Great: *cf.* IX.43.7

Alexis, supposedly a boy slave
of Maecenas, who gave him
to Virgil: V.16. VI.68. VII.29.
VIII.55.12; 73

Alexis, boy slave: VIII.63

*Alfius (?) Athenagoras: IX.95.
v. Athenagoras

Algidus, adj. from Algidus,
mountainous district south
of Tusculum: X.30.6

*Almo: X.91

Almo, rivulet in the Roman
Campagna: III.47.2

Alpheus, river in the western
Peloponnese, where the
Olympic games were held:
VI.85

Altinum, coast town in Venetia:
IV.25. XIV.155

Amazon, *i.e.* Hippolyte (or
Melanippe), queen of the
Amazons, subdued by
Hercules, who took her
girdle: IX.101.5

Amazonicus, boy slave of
Flaccus: IV.42

Amazonis, epic poem by
Marsus: IV.29

[Amillus]: *v.* Hamillus

Amiternus, adj. from
Amiternum, town in the
Sabine country: XIII.20

*Ammianus: II.4; 17. IV.70

*Amoenus: XII.66

Amor: VIII.50.13

*Amphion, boy: XII.75

Amphitheatrum (the
Coliseum): Sp.1; 2; 30. IX.68

Amyclae, town in Laconia:
IX.103
    Amyclaeus, adj.:
VIII.28.9. IX.72. XIV.161

Amyclae (Fundanae), town
south of Fundi (Fondi):
XIII.115

*Amyntas: XI.41

Anchialus, town in Cilicia,
founded by Sardanapalus
and containing his tomb:
XI.94

Anci, *i.e.* Ancus Marcius, fourth
king of Rome: IX.27

Andraemon, a racehorse: X.9

*Andragoras: VI.53

Andromache, wife of Hector of
Troy: III.76. V.53. *cf.*
II.41.14. X.90.6

Andromeda, princess exposed
to a sea monster and rescued
by Perseus: Sp.32.10

Anna Perenna, grove of:
IV.64.17

Annaeus Serenus, friend of
Seneca: VII.45. VIII.81

*Annianus: VI.92

*Annius: VII.48

Antaeus, Libyan giant, killed
by Hercules in a wrestling
match: XIV.48. *cf.* V.65.3.
IX.101.4

Antenoreus, adj. from Antenor
the Trojan, founder of
Patavium (Padua); hence,
Patavian: I.76. IV.25

*Antiochus, barber: XI.84

*Antiope: I.92

Antipolitanus, adj. from
Antipolis (Antibes), town in
Narbonese Gaul: IV.88.
XIII.103

339

INDEX OF NAMES

341

INDEX OF NAMES

INDEX OF NAMES

347

INDEX OF NAMES

Dulichius, adj. from Dulichium, one of the Ionian islands, often = Ithacan: XI.69

Earinus Flavius, favorite young freedman of Domitian: *cf.* IX.11; 12; 13; 16; 17; 36

Egeria, water goddess, wife of Numa, with grotto at the Porta Capena, also at Aricia: X.35.13; 68. *cf.* VI.47

"Eiarinus": IX.11.13

Elephantis, authoress of pornographical writings including an illustrated book of the varieties of copulation: XII.43

Elpenor, follower of Ulysses, who was killed falling off the roof of Circe's palace when drunk: XI.82

Elysium, abode of the blessed in the underworld: VII.14 Elysius, adj.: I.93. VI.58. VII.40. X.24; 101. XI.5.6. XII.52. Elysii (campi): IX.51.5

Emerita (Merida), city in southwest Spain: I.61.10

Encolpos, boy slave of Aulus Pudens: I.31. V.48

Endymion, young man loved by the Moon, said to be sleeping forever on Mt. Latmos: X.4

Ennius, Quintus, father of Roman poetry (239–169): V.10.7

Entellus, Domitian's freedman and secretary, party to his assassination in 96: VIII.68

Enyo, Greek war goddess, hence = warfare: Sp.27. VI.32

Eous, eastern, adj. from Eos, Dawn: III.65: VIII.26; 36

Ephesos: city on the west coast of Anatolia: X.68. *cf.* Sp.1.3

Epicurus, Athenian philosopher (342–270): *cf.* VII.69.3. X.33.2

Erigone, whose dog Maera led her to her murdered father's body: XI.69

*Eros: VII.10. X.56; 80

Erotion, lamented little slave girl of M.'s: V.34; 37. X.61

Erymanthus, mountain range in Arcadia, home of dreaded boar killed by Hercules: XI.69. *cf.* Sp.32.4. V.65.2,10. IX.101.6

Erythraeus, adj. from *Erythrum mare*, Red (*i.e.* Arabian) Sea: V.37. VIII.26; 28.14. IX.2; 12. X.17. XIII.100

Eryx, Sicilian king, son of Venus, killed by Hercules in a boxing match: II.84. V.65.4

Esquiliae, Esquiline, one of the seven hills of Rome: V.22. VII.73

Etrusci, Etruscans: X.68. *v.* Tusci Etruscus, adj.: XIII.30

Etruscus, Claudius, father and son. The father, originally a slave from Smyrna, served successive emperors, becoming head of the imperial treasury under Nero. Banished by Domitian to Campania, he was later allowed to return and died at a great age in 92. His son

INDEX OF NAMES

accompanied him in exile. His baths are eulogized also by Statius (*Silv.* 1.5), who further wrote a lament for the father's death (*Silv.* 3.3): VI.42.1; 83. VII.40

Euboica Sibylla, the Sibyl of Cumae (colony of Calchis in Euboea), a seeress who lived for many centuries: IX.29

*Euclides: V.35

*Euctus (*v.l.* Auctus): VIII.6.1. XI.28

Euganeus, adj. from Euganei, a people of northeast Italy, Venetian: IV.25. X.93. XIII.89

Euhadne (Evadne), immolated herself on the pyre of her husband Capaneus: IV.75

*Eulogus, auctioneer: VI.8

Euphemus: Domitian's butler: IV.8

Europa, continent: V.74

Europe, daughter of Agenor, king of Tyre, carried overseas to Crete by Jupiter in the guise of a bull: Sp.19. XIV.180.*lemm.* Portico of same: II.14.3,5, 15: III.20.12. *cf.* VII.32.12. XI.1.11

Eurotas, Sparta's river: IX.75

Eurydice, wife of Orpheus, the wonder-musician, *q.v.*: Sp.25. XIV.165

Eurystheus, king of Mycenae, under whose orders Hercules performed his labors: IX.65.7

*Eutrapelus (barber): VII.83

Eutychos, boy slave of

Castricus, lamented by M.: VI.68

Evadne: *v.* Euhadne

*Fabianus: III.36. IV.5; 24. XII.83

Fabii, ancient Roman clan: VI.64.1. VII.58

*Fabius: VII.66. VIII.43. IX.8

Fabricia: XI.2

Fabricius Luscinus, C., third-century general and, like his contemporary Curius, type of old Roman virtue: VII.68. X.73. XI.5.8; 16. Fabricii: IX.28. *cf.* XI.2

Fabricius, Chief Centurion: I.93

*Fabulla: I.64. II.41.11. IV.81. VI.12. VIII.33.17; 79. *v.* Labulla

*Fabullinus: XII.51

*Fabullus: III.12.IV.87. V.35. VI.72. IX.66. XI.35. XII.20; 22; 85

Faenius Telesphorus, father of Antulla: I.114; 116

Falernum (-na), premier Italian wine from northern Campania: I.18; 71; 106. II.40. III.77. V.64. VI.27. VII.27. VIII.55.14; 77. IX.22; 73; 93. X.36; 66. XI.8; 26; 36; 49. XII.17; 70. XIII.108; 111. XIV.113; 170
    Falernus, adj.: XII.57.22. XIII.120

Faliscus, adj. from Falerii in Etruria: IV.46.8

Fama, the goddess Fame or Rumor: Sp.1; 6; 8; 19. I.25; 29. VII.6; 12. VIII.3.4

INDEX OF NAMES

357

INDEX OF NAMES

INDEX OF NAMES

INDEX OF NAMES

INDEX OF NAMES

365

INDEX OF NAMES

Massa, thief: XII.28.2 (*v.* note)

Massica, wine from Mt.
Massicus in Campania:
III.26; 49. IV.69. XIII.111
Massicus, adj.: I.26. IV.13

Massilia (Marseilles): X.36.
XIII.123. XIV.118.
Massilitanum, wine:
XIII.123.*lemm.*
Massilitanus, adj.:
III.82.23

Massylus, adj. from Massyli, a
people of Numidia: VIII.53.
IX.22; 71 X.94. XIII.37

Mater, the Great Mother
(Mater Magna), Cybele:
III.47.2. V.41.3. XIV.204

Maternus, jurist, native of
Bilbilis, old friend of M.:
I.96. II.74. X.37.3

*Matho: IV.79. VI.33. VII.10;
90. VIII.42. X.46. XI.68

*Matrinia (*v.l.* Matronia):
III.32

[Matro]: *v.* Maro

Mattiacus, adj.: XIV.27 (see
note)

Maurici, *i.e.* M. Junius
Mauricus, senator, banished
by Domitian in 93. Recalled
in 97, he became a member
of Trajan's Advisory Council
(*consilium*). A model of fair
dealing· V.28

Maurus, Moor: VI.39.6. Mauri:
X.6
Maurus, adj.: IX.22.
XIV.90. Maurusiacus, adj.:
XII.66

Mausolus, King of Caria (d.
353), whose wife Artemisia
built him a tomb which

ranked among the seven
wonders of the world and
gave its name to the
Mausoleum of Augustus:
X.63. Mausolea, (a) tomb of
Mausolus: Sp.1. (b)
Mausoleum of Augustus:
V.64

*Maximina: II.41

Maximus: *v.* Caesonius, Vibius

*Maximus: I.69. II.18; 53.
III.18. V.70. VII.73. X.77

Medea: *v.* Colchis

Medusaeus, adj. from Medusa:
VII.1. *v.* Gorgon

Megalensis, adj. from
Megale(n)sia, festival in
honor of the Great (Megalê)
Mother Cybele, held in
April: X.41

Megara, wife of Hercules: XI.43

Melaenis, poetical mistress of
Marsus: VII.29

*Melanthio: X.67

Meleagros, Meleager, who
killed the Calydonian boar:
Sp.17

Melior, M. Atedius, a rich
patron of M. and Statius
(*Silv.* 2.1): II.69. IV.54.
VI.28; 29. VIII.38

Melpomene, a Muse: IV.31

Memmii, *i.e.* C. Memmius
Regulus, consul in A.D. 63:
XII.36

Memnon, son of the dawn
goddess Aurora: VIII.21

Memor, author of tragedies,
brother of the satirist
Turnus: XI.9; 10

Memphis, Egyptian city: Sp.1.
VII.99. VIII.36

367

Roman, who tried to kill
Porsenna and when
captured put his hand in the
fire to show his indifference
to pain: I.21. X.25. Mucii:
VI.19 (*v.* note). *cf.* VIII.30

Mulvius *or* Mulvius pons,
bridge across the Tiber north
of Rome: III.14. IV.64.23

Munatius Gallus: X.33

*Munna: IX.82. X.36; 60

Musa, the nine Muses presided
over the arts: II.22.2. III.20.
IV.49. VIII.3. IX.26. X.18.
XII.11. Musae: I.12. II.41.21;
89; 92. IV.31. V.6. VII.8; 46;
63. VIII.82. IX.11.17; 58; 99.
X.58. XI.1; 93. XIII.1. *v.*
Aonides, Camenae, Castalis,
Pierides, Pipleis. Also called
the Nine Sisters or the
Poetic (*doctae*) Sisters:
I.76.3. II.22. V.6.18. IX.42.3

Mussetius, unknown
pornographer: XII.95

Mutina (Modena), town in
northern Italy: III.59

Mycenae, ancient city in
Argolis, scene of much
legendary evildoing: IV.55.5.
XIV.1

Myrīni campi, plain of Myrina
(town in Mysia), site of the
oracle of Grynean Apollo:
IX.42

Myrīnus, gladiator and beast
fighter: Sp.23. XII.28.7

Myron, of Athens, fifth-century
sculptor and engraver:
IV.39. VI.92. VIII.50.1

*Myrtale: V.4

Mys, fifth-century engraver:

VIII.34; 50.1. XIV.95

*Naevia: I.68; 106. II.9; 26.
III.13 (?)

*Naevolus: I.97. II.46. III.71;
95. IV.83. *cf.* III.13 (note)

Nais, Naiad, a water nymph:
VII.15. Naides: VI.68

*Nanneius: V.14. XI.61

Narbo, Narbo Paterna
(Narbonne): city of southern
Gaul. Refounded as a colony
(Colonia Julia) by Julius
Caesar, it later became
officially Col. Iulia Paterna
Narbo Martius: VIII.72

Narnia (Narni), town in
Umbria: VII.93

*Nasica: II.79. XI.28

*Nasidianus (*v.l.* -ienus):
VII.54

Naso: *v.* Ovidius

*Nasta: IX.87

*Natta: XI.72

Natura: XI.80

Nausicaa, daughter of
Alcinous: XII.31

Neapolis (Naples): V.78.14

Nemee, Nemea, valley in
Argolis, haunt of a dreaded
lion killed by Hercules: Sp.8;
32.3. V.65.2. IX.71. *cf,*
IX.101.6
    Nemeaeus, adj.: IV.57.
    V.65.9

Nemesis, Tibullus' second
poetic mistress: VIII.73.
XIV.193 (by mistake for
Delia)

Nepos, friend and neighbor of
M.: VI.27. X.48.5. XIII.124

Neptunus: cf. Sp.19.1; 34.6

369

INDEX OF NAMES

INDEX OF NAMES

INDEX OF NAMES

INDEX OF NAMES

INDEX OF NAMES

INDEX OF NAMES

INDEX OF NAMES